TWINKIE CHAN'S
CROCHETED ABODE
À LA MODE

Quarto is the authority on a wide range of topics.

Quarto educates, entertains and enriches the lives of our readers—enthusiasts and lovers of hands-on living.

www.quartoknows.com

© 2016 Quarto Publishing Group USA Inc.
Text and photographs © 2016 Twinkie Chan Inc.
Illustrations © 2016 Candace Okamura

First published in the United States of America in 2016 by
Creative Publishing international, an imprint of

Quarto Publishing Group USA Inc.
400 First Avenue North
Suite 400
Minneapolis, MN 55401
1-800-328-3895

quartoknows.com
Visit our blogs at quartoknows.com

10 9 8 7 6 5 4 3 2 1

ISBN: 978-1-58923-930-2

Digital edition published in 2016
eISBN: 978-1-63159-154-9

Library of Congress Cataloging-in-Publication Data available

Design and page layout: Laura Shaw Design Inc.
Photography: Stephanie Lee
Illustration: Candace Okamura
Technical editor: Lori Steinberg

Printed in China

TWINKIE CHAN'S
CROCHETED ABODE
À LA MODE

❋

20 YUMMY CROCHET PROJECTS FOR YOUR HOME

Creative Publishing international

contents

kitchen & dining

living & lounging

bath & beauty

home office

introduction

Throw some rainbow mini pompoms in the air! We're going to cover your home in cute, colorful, scrumptious crochet! You won't find a single granny afghan or lace doily in this book, but you *will* find ottomans shaped like donuts, aprons that look like honey bears, and the biggest, squishiest, yummiest banana split throw pillow you've ever seen.

My first book, *Twinkie Chan's Crochet Goodies for Fashion Foodies,* focused on my signature food-themed scarves to keep you cozy. Since then, I've started selling patterns on Etsy, sharing free patterns on my blog, and also filming crochet tutorials on YouTube. I've worked with awesome companies like Michaels Stores, the Craft Yarn Council, Lion Brand Yarns, and Lily Sugar 'n Cream to help with various yarn launches and promos, and I've gotten a great response to the home decor crochet projects I've created. So I wanted to dedicate this book to keeping your home cozy. I take the plushy adorableness of amigurumi and turn that into a useful item for your house, so that all your hard work doesn't just sit on a shelf looking precious, but actually becomes part of your everyday life.

Crochet innately has a nostalgic, comfy, home-y feeling, and I hope to help you kick that crochet into cute with these twenty yummy projects. If you're new to crocheting or need a refresher on basic techniques, skip to the guide at the back of the book. Otherwise, you can jump right in and find all the ingredients and guidance you need for your future crocheted abode à la mode!

kitchen & dining

Get ready to be the crochet host(ess) with the most(est)!
We're going to amp up the yummy-factor in your kitchen with
some dessert-themed cozies, breakfast-themed accessories,
and even a lil something sweet to wear yourself!

Hungry yet? Let's dive in!

strawberry shortcake stand-mixer cover

I'm currently borrowing my mother's stand-mixer, and it lives next to a window in my kitchen that overlooks my garden. I have this window open quite a bit, and the mixer is sporting a fine coat of garden dirt. This is a crochet-cozy 911 situation! I'm known to start whipping up baked goods at three o'clock in the morning, and skipping the decontamination process would be a huge bonus. If you follow my work, you know that I have a habit of turning all objects into cakes by covering them in cake-shaped cozies, and this strawberry shortcake mixer cover is no exception! I'm topping my pink frosting with whipped cream and berries, but you can have all kinds of fun choosing your own colors, flavors, and decorations!

INGREDIENTS

 worsted weight

Red Heart Super Saver Economy, acrylic, 7 oz (198 g)/364 yds (333 m) per skein: 1 skein each #0706 Perfect Pink (A), #0320 Cornmeal (B), #0311 White (C), #0724 Baby Pink (D), #0319 Cherry Red (E)

5mm mini pompoms in assorted colors

small amount of polyester stuffing

TOOLS

H/8 (5.00 mm) crochet hook

tapestry needle

stitch marker

straight pins

fabric glue

fabric hot glue and glue gun for attaching strawberries (optional) plus aluminum foil and piece of cardboard to keep hot glue from seeping through

DIRECTIONS

Gauge

15 sts x 13 rnds in hdc = 4" (10 cm).
Take time to check gauge.

Finished Size

38" (96.5 cm) circumference, at widest point x 18"
(45.5 cm) long, excluding strawberries

Note: Sample fits a KitchenAid K5SS stand-mixer with a 5-quart bowl

Special Stitches Used

HALF DOUBLE CROCHET 2 TOGETHER (HDC2TOG)
[Yo, insert hook in next st, yo and draw up a loop] twice, yo and draw yarn through all 5 loops on hook.

Notes:
1. Cover is worked from the top down in an oval shape.
2. The 1st hdc of each rnd is worked in the same st as joining st from the previous rnd.

Frosting, Cake, and Filling

With A, ch 26.

Rnd 1: (3 hdc) in 3rd ch, hdc in next 22 sts, (5 hdc) in next ch; working in other side of foundation ch, hdc in next 22 sts, (2 hdc) in last ch, join with sl st in 1st hdc, turn—54 hdc. Place marker for beg of rnd.

Rnd 2: Ch 2, (2 hdc) in next 3 hdc, hdc in next 22 hdc, (2 hdc) in next 5 hdc, hdc in next 22 hdc, (2 hdc) in next 2 hdc, join with sl st in 1st hdc, turn—64 hdc.

Rnd 3: Ch 2, hdc in next st, [(2 hdc) in next hdc, hdc in next st] twice, hdc in next 22 hdc, [(2 hdc) in next hdc, hdc in next hdc] 5 times, hdc in next 22 hdc, [(2 hdc) in next hdc, hdc in next st] twice, (2 hdc) in next hdc, join with sl st in 1st hdc, turn—74 hdc.

Rnd 4: Ch 2, hdc in next 2 hdc, [(2 hdc) in next hdc, hdc in next 2 hdc] twice, hdc in next 22 hdc, [(2 hdc) in next hdc, hdc in next 2 hdc] 5 times, hdc in next 22 hdc, [(2 hdc) in next hdc, hdc in next 2 hdc] twice, (2 hdc) in next hdc, join with sl st in 1st hdc, turn—84 hdc.

Rnd 5: Ch 2, hdc in next 2 hdc, [(2 hdc) in next hdc, hdc in next 3 hdc] twice, 22 hdc, [(2 hdc) in next hdc, hdc in next 3 hdc] 5 times, hdc in next 22 hdc, [(2 hdc) in next hdc, hdc in next 3 hdc] twice, (2 hdc) in next hdc, hdc in next hdc, join with sl st in 1st hdc, turn—94 hdc.

Rnd 6: Ch 2, hdc in next 3 hdc, [(2 hdc) in next hdc, hdc in next 4 hdc] twice, hdc in next 22 hdc, [(2 hdc) in next hdc, hdc in next 4 hdc] 5 times, 22 hdc, [(2 hdc), 4 hdc] [(2 hdc) in next hdc, hdc in next 4 hdc] twice, (2 hdc) in next hdc, hdc in next hdc, join with sl st in 1st hdc, turn—104 hdc.

Rnd 7: Ch 2, hdc in each st around, join with sl st in 1st hdc, turn.

Rnd 8: Ch 2, hdc in next 3 hdc, [(2 hdc) in next hdc, hdc in next 5 hdc] twice, hdc in next 22 hdc, [(2 hdc) in next hdc, hdc in next 5 hdc] 5 times, 22 hdc, [(2 hdc) in next hdc, hdc in next 5 hdc] 2 times, (2 hdc) in next hdc, hdc in next 2 hdc, join with sl st in 1st hdc, turn—114 hdc.

Rnds 9–11: Ch 2, hdc in each st around, join with sl st in 1st hdc, turn.

Rnd 12: Ch 2, [(2 hdc) in next hdc, hdc in next 6 hdc] twice, hdc in next 36 hdc, [(2 hdc) in next hdc, hdc in next 6 hdc] 3 times, hdc in next 36 hdc, (2 hdc) in next hdc, hdc in next 6 hdc, join with sl st in 1st hdc, turn—120 hdc.

Rnds 13–17: Ch 2, hdc in each st around, join with sl st in 1st hdc, turn.

Rnd 18 (scallops): Ch 1, with RS facing and working in FLO, [sk 2 sts, (7 tr) in next st, sk 2 sts, sl st in next st] 20 times, join with sl st in 1st hdc, turn—20 scallops.

Rnd 19: Ch 1, with WS facing and working in the remaining loops of rnd 17, (**see Photo 1**), sc in each hdc around, join with sl st in 1st hdc, turn—120 hdc. Fasten off A.

Rnd 20: With B, working in both loops of rnd 19, hdc in each hdc around, turn.

Rnds 21–24: Rep rnd 7. Fasten off B.

Rnd 25: With C, ch 2, [(2 hdc) in next hdc, hdc in next 12 hdc] twice, hdc in next 21 hdc, [(2 hdc) in next hdc, hdc in next 12 hdc] 3 times, hdc in next 21 hdc, (2 hdc) in next hdc, hdc in next 12 hdc, join with sl st in 1st hdc, turn—126 hdc.

Rnds 26–28: Ch 2, hdc in each st around, join with sl st in 1st hdc, turn.

Rnd 29: Ch 2, [(2 hdc) in next hdc, hdc in next 16 hdc] twice, hdc in next 12 hdc, [(2 hdc) in next hdc, hdc in next 16 hdc] 3 times, hdc in next 12 hdc, (2 hdc) in next hdc, hdc in next 16 hdc, join with sl st in 1st hdc, turn—132 hdc.

Rnd 30: Ch 2, hdc in each st around, join with sl st in 1st hdc, turn. Fasten off C.

Rnds 31–32: With B, ch 2, hdc in each st around, join with sl st in 1st hdc, turn.

Rnd 33: Ch 2, [(2 hdc) in next hdc, hdc in next 17 hdc] twice, hdc in next 12 hdc, [(2 hdc) in next hdc, hdc in next 17 hdc] 3 times, hdc in next 12 hdc, (2 hdc) in next hdc, hdc in next 17 hdc, join with sl st in 1st hdc, turn—138 hdc.

Rnd 34: Ch 2, hdc in each st around, join with sl st in 1st hdc, turn. Fasten off B.

Rnd 35: With C, ch 2, hdc in each st around, join with sl st in 1st hdc, turn. (138)

(continued)

For a mixer with bowl lift handle only:

Rnd 36: Ch 2, hdc in next 22 hdc, ch 4 loosely, sk 4 sts for handle opening, hdc in rem hdc around—138.

For a mixer with no bowl lift handle only:

Rnd 36: Ch 2, hdc in each st around, join with sl st in 1st hdc, turn.

For all mixers:

Rnd 37: Ch 2, hdc in next 42 hdc, [(2 hdc) in next hdc, hdc in next 17 hdc] 3 times, (2 hdc) in next hdc, hdc in next 41 hdc, sl st to 1st hdc to join, turn join with sl st in 1st hdc, turn—142 hdc.

Rnds 38-40: Rep rnd 7. Fasten off C.

Rnds 41-44: With B, rep rnd 7.

Rnd 45: With C, ch 2, [hdc2tog, hdc in next 19 hdc] twice, hdc in next 8 hdc, [hdc2tog, hdc in next 19 hdc] 3 times, hdc in next 8 hdc, hdc2tog, hdc in next 19 hdc, join with sl st in 1st hdc, turn—136.

Rnds 46-50: Ch 2, hdc in each st around, join with sl st in 1st hdc, turn. Fasten off C.

Rnds 51-54: With B, ch 2, hdc in each st around, join with sl st in 1st hdc, turn. Fasten off B.

Rnd 55: With A, ch 2, hdc in each st around, join with sl st in 1st hdc, turn.

Rnd 56: Ch 2, [hdc2tog, hdc in next 18 hdc] twice, hdc in next 8 hdc, [hdc2tog, hdc in next 18 hdc] 3 times, hdc in next 8 hdc, hdc2tog, hdc in next18 hdc, join with sl st in 1st hdc, turn.

Rnd 57: Ch 2, hdc in each st around, join with sl st in 1st hdc, turn.

Rnd 58: Ch 1, sc in next 5 sts, [sc2tog, sc in next 9 sts] twice, sc in next 21 sts, [sc2tog, sc in next 9 sts] 4 times, sc in next 21 sts, sc2tog, sc in next 9 sts, sc2tog, sc in next 4 sts, join with sl st in 1st sc—122 sc. Fasten off.

Strawberry Slice (make 30)

With D, ch 3, join with sl st to form ring. Place marker for beg of rnd.

Rnd 1: Ch 2, 5 hdc in ring, turn—5 hdc.

Rnd 2: Ch 1 (2 sc) in each st, turn—10 sc. Fasten off D, leaving approx 12" (30.5 cm) for sewing.

Rnd 3: Join E, ch 1, sc in next 2 sc, (2 sc) in next sc, sc, (2 sc) in next 2 sc, sc in next sc, (2 sc) in next sc, sc in next 2 sc—14 sc. Fasten off, leaving approx 18" (45.5 cm) for sewing.

With RS of strawberry slice facing and C, work surface sl st or embroidered chain st between rnds 1 and 2.

Whole Strawberry (make 3)

*Notes: Do **not** join rnds. RS of work is outside of strawberry.*

With E, ch 3, join with sl st to form ring. Place marker for beg of rnd.

Rnd 1: Ch 1, work 6 sc in ring—6 sc.

Rnd 2: (2 sc) in each sc around—12 sc.

Rnd 3: [(2 sc) in next sc, sc in next sc] 6 times around—18 sc.

Rnd 4: [(2 sc) in next sc, sc in next 2 sc] 6 times around—24 sc.

Rnd 5: Sc in each sc around.

Rnd 6: [invdec, sc in next 10 sc] twice—22 sc.

Rnd 7: Sc in each sc around.

Rnd 8: [invdec, sc in next 9 sc] twice—20 sc.

Rnd 9: Sc in each sc around.

Rnd 10: [invdec, sc in next 8 sc] twice—18 sc.

Rnd 11: [invdec, sc in next 4 sc] 3 times—15 sc.

Rnd 12: [invdec, sc in next 3 sc] 3 times—12 sc.

Stuff with polyester stuffing.

Rnd 13: [invdec, 2 sc] 3 times, sl st to next st to join—9 sc.

Fasten off leaving 1 yd (1 m) for sewing later.

With tapestry needle, weave yarn tail through outer loops of rem 9 sts and pull to close. Tie off and save end for sewing.

Whipped Cream (make 3)

With C, ch 42.

Row 1: Sk 1st 2 ch, then work (2 dc) in each rem ch—80 sts.

Fasten off, leaving 1 yd (1 m) for sewing later.

Assembly

With 1 yd (1 m) of A at a time, sew edges of frosting scallops down so they don't flip up.

ATTACH STRAWBERRY SLICES

Pin 10 strawberry slices to the top white stripe, spacing them evenly around. Sew using the tails, or hot glue slices in place. Rep for the other white stripes, using the photo as a guide. If gluing, use aluminum foil and/or cardboard to protect surfaces from glue.

ATTACH WHOLE STRAWBERRIES

Weave the long tails of each whole strawberry away from the strawberry center. Place the cover on the stand-mixer and pin the strawberries to the top of the cover, evenly spaced. Using the long tails, sew the outer strawberries in place. Then, sew the center strawberry in place. If using hot glue to attach the strawberries, first cover the top of the mixer with aluminum foil to prevent getting glue on mixer.

WHIPPED CREAM

Wrap 1 whipped cream ruffle around the base of each whole strawberry. Pin and sew down using yarn tails.

RAINBOW SPRINKLES

With fabric glue, attach mini pompoms, using photo as guide.

grocery fridge magnets

My fridge is where I like to collect all my photo booth pictures with friends, and I need a ton of magnets! These grocery-themed magnets are a fun way to keep your keepsakes and to-do lists in order. Plus, you'll get a lot of mileage out of these little guys because you can also turn them into hair clips or brooches! I use a lot of Cascade 220 for these magnets because it comes in a super wide range of colors and is a nice, light worsted weight, but if you want your grocery foods to turn out bigger or smaller, you can just adjust your yarn weight and your hook size.

INGREDIENTS

(4) worsted weight

Steak: Cascade 220: 12 yds (11 m) #8414 Bright Red (A)
and 8 yds (8 m) #8010 Natural (B)

Fish: Cascade 220: 10 yds (9 m) #8401 Silver Grey (A);
Lion Brand Vanna's Choice: small amount #860-151
Charcoal Gray (B)

Baguette: Cascade 220: 10 yds (9 m) #2415 Sunflower (A)
and 3 yds (3 m) #8412 Pear (B)

Soup Can: Cascade 220: 8 yds (8 m) #8401 Silver Grey (A),
3 yds (3 m) #8414 Bright Red (B), and 4 yds (4 m) #8505
White (C); Lion Brand Vanna's Glamour (sport weight yarn:
2 yds (2 m) #861-171 Gold (D); Lion Brand Vanna's Choice:
1 yd (1 m) #860-151 Charcoal Gray (E)

Broccoli: Cascade 220: 16 yds (15 m) #8910 Citron (A)
and 15 yds (14 m) #2409 Palm (B)

Donut: Cascade 220: 15 yds (14 m) #8412 Pear (A) and 6 yds
(6 m) #9478 Cotton Candy (B); small amount of various
colored yarn for sprinkles

Can of Ham: Cascade 220: 8 yds (8 m) #7818 Blue Velvet (A),
2 yds (2 m) #9478 Cotton Candy (B), and 2 yds (2 m)
#7827 Goldenrod (C); Lion Brand Vanna's Glamour (sport
weight yarn: 3 yds (3 m) #861-171 Gold (D)

Fried Egg: Cascade 220: 10 yds (9 m) #8505 White (A)
and 2 yds (2m) #7827 Goldenrod (B)

Lemon: Cascade 220: 10 yds (9 m) #7827 Goldenrod (A)
and 1 yd (1 m) #8903 Primavera (B)

TOOLS

G/6 (4.00 mm) crochet hook

tapestry needle

polyester stuffing

¾" (2 cm) ceramic magnets from the craft store

hot glue or craft glue

STEAK MAGNET

Gauge (for all)

15 sts x 18 rows in sc = 4" (10 cm).
Take time to check gauge.

Finished Size

Approx 2.75" (7 cm) x 2.5" (5 cm)

Steak Front

With A, ch 5.

Row 1: Sc in 2nd ch from hook, sc in next 3 ch, turn—4 sc.

Row 2: Ch 1, sc in each sc across, turn.

Row 3: Ch 1, (2 sc) in 1st sc, sc in next 3 sc, turn—5 sc.

Row 4: Ch 1, sc in each sc across, turn.

Row 5: Ch 1, (2 sc) in 1st sc, sc in next 4 sc, turn—6 sc.

Row 6: Ch 1, (2 sc) in 1st sc, sc in next 5 sc, turn—7 sc.

Row 7: Ch 1, (2 sc) in 1st sc, sc in next 6 sc, turn—8 sc.

Row 8: Ch 1, (2 sc) in 1st sc, sc in next 7 sc, turn—9 sc.

Row 9: Ch 1, sc in next 8 sc, (2 sc) in next sc, turn—10 sc.

Row 10: Ch 1, sc in each sc across, turn.

Row 11: Ch 1, [sc2tog] twice, sc in next 4 sc, sc2tog, turn—7 sc.

Row 12: Ch 1, sc2tog, sc in next 3 sc, sc2tog—5 sc. Fasten off
and weave in ends.

Steak Back

Work rows 1–12 as for steak front. Fasten off A. Join B with sl st,
turn.

Work 1 rnd of sc evenly around steak back, sl st to 1st sc to join,
turn—32 sc.

Next rnd: Ch 1, sc in each sc around, sl st to 1st sc to join. Fasten
off, leaving a tail 1 yd (1 m) long for sewing, and weave in
other end.

T-Bone

With B, ch 7.

Row 1: Sl st in 2nd ch from hook, sl st in next 2 ch, ch 10 (for long
part of T), turn, sl st in 2nd ch from hook, sl st each ch to end.

Fasten off, leaving a tail 18" (45 cm) long for sewing.

17

(continued)

Assembly

Sew T-Bone to steak front.

With T-Bone facing out, place steak front on top of steak back. With long tail of steak back, sew front to back using double whipstitches, making sure to match up the shapes. Stuff lightly while sewing. Complete sewing closed and weave in ends.

Glue magnet to back of piece.

FISH MAGNET

Finished Size

Approx 3.5" (9 cm) x 1.5" (3 cm)

Fish Side (Make 2)

With A, ch 2.

Row 1: (3 sc) in 2nd ch, turn—3 sc.

Row 2: Ch 1, sc in each sc across, turn.

Row 3: Ch 1, (2 sc) in 1st sc, sc in next, (2 sc) in next sc, turn—5 sc.

Row 4: Ch 1, sc in each sc across, turn.

Row 5: Ch 1, sc in next 2 sc, (2 sc) in next sc, sc in next 2 sc, turn—6 sc.

Rows 6-9: Ch 1, sc in each sc across, turn.

Row 10: Ch 1, sc in next 2 sc, sc2tog, sc in next 2 sc, turn—5 sc.

Row 11: Ch 1, sc in each sc across, turn.

Row 12: Ch 1, sc in next 2 sc, sc2tog, sc in next sc, turn—4 sc.

Row 13: Ch 1, sc in each sc across, turn.

Row 14: Ch 1, sc in 1st sc, sc2tog, sc in next sc, turn—3 sc.

Row 15: Ch 1, sc in each sc across, turn.

Row 16: Ch 3, htr in 1st sc, ch 3, sl st in next st, ch 3, (1 htr, ch 3, sl st) in next sc.

Fasten off and weave in ends. When 2nd fish side is complete, fasten off, leaving a tail 24" (61 cm) long for sewing.

Assembly

With B, thread tapestry needle, and using photo as guide, embroider an eye, mouth, gill, and scales on 1st side.

Place 2nd fish side behind the embroidered side and whipstitch the 2 sides together. Stuff lightly before sewing is complete.

Glue magnet to back.

BAGUETTE MAGNET

Finished Size

Approx 3.5" (9 cm) x 1" (2.5 cm)

*Notes: Do **not** join rnds, rather work in a continuous spiral. RS is outside of baguette.*

Baguette

With A, ch 3, join with sl st to form ring. Place marker for beg of rnd.

Rnd 1: Work 6 sc in ring.

Rnd 2: (2 sc) in each sc around—12 sc.

Rnds 3-18: Sc in each sc around. Baguette measures approx 3" (7.5 cm) long. Stuff lightly.

Rnd 19: [invdec] 6 times. Sl st in next st—6 sts.

Fasten off, leaving a tail 8" (12.5 cm) long for sewing. Weave tail through rem 6 sts and pull to close. Weave in ends.

Assembly

With tapestry needle, 1 yd (1 m) of B at a time, and using photo as guide, use 3 or 4 sts each to embroider diagonal slits along baguette, working sts through all the layers of fabric and stuffing to mimic the slightly indented slits on a real baguette.

Glue magnet to back.

SOUP CAN MAGNET

Finished Size

Approx 1.75" (4.5 cm) x 2.25" (5.5 cm)

Can Front

With A, ch 7.

Rnd 1: Sc in 2nd ch from hook, sc in next 4 ch, (3 sc) in last ch, working in opposite side of foundation ch, sc in next 4 sc, (2 sc) in last ch, sl st to 1st sc to join—14 sc. Fasten off A. Join B in last sl st in rnd 1.

Row 1: Ch 1, sc2tog (same st as joining and next sc), (2 sc) in next sc, sc in next 2 sc, (2 sc) in next sc, sc2tog, turn—8 sc.

Rows 2-4: Ch 1, sc2tog, (2 sc) in next sc, sc in next 2 sc, (2 sc) in next sc, sc2tog, turn—8 sc.

Fasten off B.

Rows 5-8: With C, rep row 2.

Fasten off and weave in all ends. Note that RS of rnd 1 is the front of can.

Can Back

With A, work as for can front, without any color changes.
Fasten off, leaving a tail 24" (61 cm) long for sewing.

Gold Label

With D, ch 2.

Rnd 1: Work (6 sc) into 2nd ch from hook, join with sl st to 1st sc—6 sc.

Fasten off leaving a tail 1 yd (1 m) long for sewing and weave in other end.

Assembly

Using photo as guide and long tail, sew gold label to center of can front.

With D, backstitch the word "SOUP" in the white portion of can.

With E, backstitch a border around the top of can front to outline the oval-shaped top of can.

With C, backstitch the word "YUM" in the red portion of can.

Place can back behind can front, whipstitch the 2 pieces together using the long tail of the back. Stuff lightly before sewing is complete.

Glue magnet to back.

BROCCOLI MAGNET

Finished size

Approx 2.75" (7 cm) x 2.75" (7 cm)

Stem (make 2)

With A, ch 6.

Row 1: Sc in 2nd ch from hook, sc in next 4 sc, turn—5 sc.

Row 2: Ch 1, sc in each sc across, turn.

Row 3: Ch 1, sc in next 2 sc, (2 sc) in next sc, sc in next 2 sc, turn—6 sc.

Row 4: Ch 1, sc in each sc across, turn.

Row 5: Ch 4, sc in 2nd sc from hook, sc in next 2 sts, sk 1st sc in row 4 and sl st in the 2nd sc, [sc in 2nd sc from hook, sc in next 2 sts, sk 1st sc in row 4 and sl st in the next st] twice.

Fasten off, leaving a tail approx 18" (45.5 cm) long for sewing, and weave in ends.

1.

Floret (Make 2)

Note: WS of work will show on the outside, so that trs create a nice, nubby texture. Do not join rnds when working floret, rather work in a continuous spiral.

With B, ch 3, join with sl st form ring. Place marker for beg of rnd.

Rnd 1: Ch 1, [tr, sc] 3 times in ring—6 sts.

Rnd 2: (Tr, sc) in each st—12 sts.

Rnd 3: [(Tr, sc) in next st, sc in next st] 6 times—18 sts.

Rnd 4: [Tr in next st, sc in next st] 9 times.

Rnd 5: [Sc2tog, sc in next st] 6 times—12 sts.

Rnd 6: [Sc2tog] 6 times, sl st to next st to join—6 sts.

Fasten off, leaving a tail 12" (30.5 cm) long. Weave through rem 6 sts and pull to close. Weave in ends.

Assembly

Place 1st stem on top of 2nd stem and sew together, stuffing lightly before sewing is complete.

Being sure that nubby side of each floret faces the front of the magnet, overlap florets so that the edge of one reaches the center of the other, and sew together. (**Photo 1**)

Place stem on top of florets, and with A, sew together, using photo as guide.

Glue magnet to back.

DONUT MAGNET

Finished Size

2.25" (5.5 cm) x 1.75" (4.5 cm)

*Note: Donut is oval-shaped rather than a perfect circle. Do **not** join rnds, rather work in a continuous spiral.*

Donut

With A, ch 12. Join with sl st to form ring, being careful not to twist ch. Place marker for beg of rnd.

Rnd 1: Ch 1, sc in each ch—12 sc.

Rnd 2: (2 sc) in next sc, sc in next 3 sc, (2 sc) in next 3 sc, sc in next 3 sc, (2 sc) in next 2 sc—18 sc.

Rnd 3: (2 sc) in next sc, sc in next 4 sc, [(2 sc) in next sc, sc in next sc] 3 times, sc in next 3 sc, [(2 sc) in next sc, sc in next sc] twice—24 sc.

Rnd 4: (2 sc) in next sc, sc in next 5 sc, [(2 sc) in next sc, sc in next 2 sc] 3 times, sc in next 3 sc, [(2 sc) in next sc, sc in next 2 sc] twice—30 sc.

Rnd 5: Sc in each sc around, sc in next 4 sc to move beg of rnd—30 sc.

Rnd 6: invdec, sc in next 5 sc, [invdec, sc in next 2 sc] 3 times, 3 sc, [invdec, sc in next 2 sc] twice—24 sc.

Rnd 7: invdec, sc in next 4 sc, [invdec, sc in next sc] 3 times, sc in next 3 sc, [invdec, sc in next sc] twice—18 sc.

Rnd 8: invdec, sc in next 3 sc, [invdec] 3 times, sc in next 3 sc, [invdec] twice, sl st to next st to join—12 sc.

Fasten off, leaving a tail 24" (61 cm) long for sewing, and weave in other end.

Frosting

With B, ch 18, leaving a tail 18" (45.5 cm) for sewing. Join with sl st to 1st ch to form ring, being careful not to twist ch. Place marker for beg of rnd.

Rnd 1: Ch 1, sc in each ch around—18 sc.

Rnd 3: (2 sc) in next sc, sc in next 4 sc, [(2 sc) in next sc, sc in next sc] 3 times, sc in next 3 sc, [(2 sc) in next sc, sc in next sc] twice—24 sc.

Rnd 4: (2 sc) in next sc, sc in next 5 sc, [(2 sc) in next sc, sc in next 2 sc] 3 times, sc in next 3 sc, [(2 sc) in next sc, sc in next 2 sc] twice, sc in last st once more, join with sl st in next st—30 sc.

Fasten off, leaving a tail 24" (61 cm) long for sewing, and weave in other end.

2.

Assembly

Place a small amount of stuffing in the center of the donut and whipstitch last rnd to foundation ch to form donut. (**Photo 2**)

Use different colors of yarn or embroidery thread to create sprinkles on RS of frosting.

Sew outer edge of frosting to top of donut. Sew inner edge of frosting to donut.

Glue magnet to back.

CAN OF HAM MAGNET

Finished Size

Approx 2" (5 cm) x 1.5" (4 cm)

Can (Make 2)

With A, ch 9.

Row 1: Sc in 2nd ch from hook, sc in each ch across, turn—8 sc.

Rows 2–7: Ch 1, sc in each sc across.

Fasten off, leaving a tail 18" (45.5 cm) long for sewing, and weave in other end.

Note: Foundation ch is the bottom of the can.

Ham

With B, ch 5.

Rnd 1: Sc in 2nd ch from hook, sc in next 2 ch, (3 sc) in last ch, working in opposite side of foundation ch, sc in next 2 ch, (2 sc) in last ch, sl st to 1st sc to join—10 sc.

Fasten off, leaving a tail 12" (30.5 cm) long for sewing, and weave in other end.

Assembly

With yarn tail, sew ham to the bottom half of one can, using photo as guide.

With C, stitch the word HAM onto the top half of the same can.

Place 2nd can behind 1st can, and sew the sides together with yarn tails, leaving top and bottom open.

With D, whipstitch the tops of the cans together, working 3-4 stitches in each crochet st to create a solid gold line across the top of the can. Stuff lightly. Then, whipstitch the bottoms of the cans together.

Glue magnet to back.

FRIED EGG MAGNET

Finished size

Approx 2" (5 cm) x 1.75" (4.5 cm)

Egg White (Make 2)

With A, ch 4.

Rnd 1: Sc in 2nd ch from hook, sc in next ch, (3 sc) in last ch, working in opposite side of foundation ch, sc in next ch, (2 sc) in last ch—8 sc. Place marker for beg of rnd.

Rnd 2: (2 sc) in 1st sc, sc in next sc, (2 sc) in next 3 sc, sc in next sc, (2 sc) in next 2 sc—14 sc.

Rnd 3: (2 sc) in 1st sc, sc in next 2 sc, [(2 sc) in next sc, sc in next sc] 3 times, sc in next sc, [(2 sc) in next sc, sc in next sc] twice, sl st to next st to join—20 sc.

Rnd 4: Sc in next sc, (2 hdc) in next 3 sc, sl st in next sc, sc in next 2 sc, (2 hdc) in next 4 sc, sc in next sc, sl st in next sc, sc in next sc, hdc in next sc, (2 hdc) in next 4 sc, sc in next sc, sl st to 1st sc to join.

Fasten off, leaving a tail 24" (61 cm) long for sewing, and weave in rem ends.

Egg Yolk

With B, ch 3, join with sl st to form ring. Place marker for beg of rnd.

Rnd 1: Ch 1, 6 sc into ring—6 sc.

Rnd 2: (2 sc) in each sc around—12 sc.

Rnd 3: Sc in each sc around, join with sl st in next st.

Fasten off, leaving a tail 18" (45.5 cm) long for sewing, and weave in other end.

Assembly

Place egg whites on top of each other, and whipstitch together. Stuff lightly before sewing is complete.

Stuff egg yolk with a scrap of B. With RS facing, sew yolk to top of egg white, using photo as guide.

Glue magnet to back.

LEMON MAGNET

Finished size

Approx 2.75" (7cm) x 1.5" (4 cm)

Note: RS shows on outside of lemon.

Lemon

With A, ch 3, join with sl st to form ring. Place marker for beg of rnd.

Rnd 1: Ch 1, work 5 sc into ring—5 sc.

Rnd 2: Sc in each sc around.

Rnd 3: (2 sc) in each sc around—10 sc.

Rnd 4: [(2 sc) in next sc, sc in next 4 sc] twice—12 sc.

Rnd 5: [(2 sc) in next sc, sc in next 3 sc] 3 times—15 sc.

Rnd 6: [(2 sc) in next sc, sc in next 4 sc] 3 times—18 sc.

Rnds 7-10: Sc in each sc around.

Rnd 11: [invdec, sc in next 4 sc] 3 times—15 sc.

Rnd 12: [invdec, sc in next 3 sc] 3 times—12 sc.

Stuff lemon lightly

Rnd 13: [invdec, sc in next 4 sc] twice—10 sc.

Rnd 14: [invdec] 5 times around—5 sc.

Rnd 15: Sc in each sc around, sl st to next st to join—5 sc.

Fasten off, leaving a tail 12" (30.5 cm) long. With tapestry needle, weave tail through rem 5 sts. Weave in ends.

Assembly

With B and tapestry needle, beg in center of first rnd, and sew 8 straight sts, working around the sts of the 1st rnd to create the nub of a stalk.

Glue magnet to back.

honey bear apron

I really love baking, even though I'm actually really bad at it! I once made a gorgeous, golden bundt cake, only to discover that it was hard as a rock! My lack of skill never stops me though, so whether you're a culinary genius or just a hopeful like me, we can still bake with style in this sweet honey bear apron. You can even leave off the arms and legs and still have an adorable piece to wear in the kitchen! Want to make one as a gift? Embroider someone's name right on the honey-bear's belly, or leave a little message, like PURE HONEY, BEE SWEET, or QUEEN BEE.

INGREDIENTS

(4) worsted weight

Lion Brand Vanna's Choice, 100% Premium Acrylic, 3.5 oz (100 g)/170 yds (156 m) per skein: 2 skeins #860-158 Mustard (A); 1 skein each #860-126 Chocolate (B) and #860-100 White (E); 8 yds (8 m) #860-113 Scarlet (D)

Premier Yarns Deborah Norville Everyday Soft Worsted, 100% Acrylic, 4 oz (113 g)/203 yds (186 m) per skein: 12 yds (11 m) #1027 Lemon (C)

TOOLS

I/9 (5.5 mm) crochet hook
tapestry needle
stitch marker
straight pins

DIRECTIONS

Gauge

14 sts x 11 rows in sc = 4" (10 cm).
Take time to check gauge.

Finished Size

15" (38 cm) wide at widest point, not including ties, x 25"
(63.5 cm) long, from top of cap to bottom of bear

Special Stitches Used

DOUBLE CROCHET 2 TOGETHER (DC2TOG)
Yo, insert hook into next stitch, yo, draw up a loop, yo, draw
through 2 loops, yo, insert hook into following st, yo and draw up
a loop, yo, draw through 2 loops, yo and draw through all 3 loops
on hook.

Notes:
1. For a slightly smaller apron, switch to a smaller hook and use a
   tighter gauge. For a child's apron, use a lighter weight worsted or a
   sport weight yarn.
2. The bear's head is an oval worked in hdc. The number of increases
   is alternated in each rnd to keep the oval flat.
3. Right and left refer to your right and left with the front of the
   honey bear facing you, rather than the honey bear's left and right.

Head

With A, ch 12.

Rnd 1: Hdc in 3rd ch from hook, hdc in next 8 ch, (5 hdc) in last
ch, working in opposite side of foundation ch, hdc in next 8
ch, (4 hdc) in last ch, join with a sl st in 1st hdc, turn—26 hdc.
Place marker for beg of rnd.

Rnd 2: Ch 2, (2 hdc) in next 4 hdc, hdc in next 8 hdc, (2 hdc) in
next 5 hdc, hdc in next 8 hdc, (2 hdc) in last hdc, join with a
sl st in 1st hdc, turn—36 hdc.

Rnd 3: Ch 2, hdc in next 11 hdc, [(2 hdc) in next hdc, hdc in next
hdc] 4 times, hdc in next 10 hdc, [(2 hdc) in next hdc, hdc in
next hdc] 3 times, (2 hdc) in last hdc, join with a sl st in 1st
hdc, turn—44 hdc.

Rnd 4: Ch 2, hdc in next hdc, [(2 hdc) in next hdc, hdc in next
2 hdc] 4 times, hdc in next 7 hdc, [(2 hdc) in next hdc, hdc
in next 2 hdc] 5 times, hdc in next 7 hdc, (2 hdc) in next hdc,
hdc in last hdc, join with a sl st in 1st hdc, turn—54 hdc.

Rnd 5: Ch 2, hdc in next 12 hdc, [(2 hdc) in next hdc, hdc in next
3 hdc] 4 times, hdc in next 12 hdc, [(2 hdc) in next hdc, hdc
in next 3 hdc] 3 times, (2 hdc) in next hdc, hdc in last hdc,
join with a sl st in 1st hdc, turn—62 hdc.

Rnd 6: Ch 2, hdc in next 2 hdc, [(2 hdc in next hdc, hdc in next
4 hdc] 4 times, hdc in next 6 hdc, [(2 hdc in next hdc, hdc in
next 4 hdc] 5 times, hdc in next 6 hdc, (2 hdc) in next hdc,
hdc in next 2 hdc, join with a sl st in 1st hdc, turn—72 hdc.

Rnd 7: Ch 2, *hdc in next 16 hdc, [(2 hdc in next hdc, hdc in next
4 hdc] 4 times; rep from * once more, join with a sl st in 1st
hdc, turn—80 hdc.

Rnd 8: Ch 2, hdc in next 4 hdc, [(2 hdc) in next hdc, hdc in next
5 hdc] 4 times, hdc in next 10 hdc, [(2 hdc) in next hdc, hdc
in next 5 hdc] 5 times, hdc in next10 hdc, (2 hdc) in next hdc,
hdc in next hdc, join with a sl st in 1st hdc, turn—90 hdc.

Rnd 9: Ch 2, hdc in next 20 hdc, [(2 hdc) in next hdc, hdc in next
5 hdc] 4 times, hdc in next 21 hdc, [(2 hdc) in next hdc, hdc
in next 5 hdc] 4 times, hdc in last hdc, join with a sl st in 1st
hdc, turn—98 hdc.

Rnd 10: Ch 2, hdc in next 6 hdc, [(2 hdc) in next hdc, hdc in next
6 hdc] 4 times, hdc in next 14 hdc, [(2 hdc) in next hdc, hdc
in next 6 hdc] 5 times, hdc in next 14 hdc, (2 hdc) in last hdc,
join with a sl st in 1st hdc, turn—108 hdc.

Rnd 11: Ch 2, hdc in next 24 hdc, [(2 hdc) in next hdc, hdc in
next 6 hdc] 4 times, hdc in next 26 hdc, [(2 hdc) in next hdc,
hdc in next 6 hdc] 4 times, hdc in next 2 hdc join with a sl st
in 1st hdc, turn—116 hdc.

Rnd 12 (RS): Ch 2, hdc in next 7 hdc, [(2 hdc) in next hdc, hdc in next 7 hdc] 4 times, hdc in next 18 hdc, [(2 hdc) in next hdc, hdc in next 7 hdc] 5 times, (2 hdc) in last hdc, join with a sl st in 1st hdc, turn—126 hdc.

Do *not* fasten off.

Left Ear

Row 1: Ch 2, hdc in same st as joining, hdc in next 9 hdc, dc in next 2 hdc, tr in next 2 hdc, turn—14 sts.

Row 2: Ch 2, sk 1 st, hdc in next 10 sts, sk next st, hdc in last st, turn—12 hdc.

Row 3: Ch 2, sk 1st hdc, hdc in next 8 hdc, sk next hdc, hdc in last hdc, turn—10 hdc.

Row 4: Ch 2, sk 1st hdc, hdc in next 6 hdc, sk next hdc, hdc in last hdc—8 hdc.

Row 5: Ch 2, sk 1st hdc, hdc in next 4 hdc, sk next hdc, hdc in last hdc—6 hdc.

Fasten off and weave in ends.

Right Ear

With the RS of head facing, starting at right side of left ear, count 34 sts (including the joining st) to the right and insert hook into the 34th st to re-join A.

Row 1: Ch 3, tr in same st as joining, tr in next hdc, dc in next 2 hdc, hdc in next 10 hdc—14 sts.

Rows 2–5: Work as for left ear. Fasten off and weave in ends.

Body

With RS of head facing, starting at left side of left ear, count 24 sts to the left and insert your hook into the 24th st to re-join A.

Row 1: Ch 2, (2 hdc) in same st as joining, hdc in next 30 sts, (2 hdc) in next st, turn—34 hdc.

Row 2: Ch 2, (2 hdc) in next 2 hdc, hdc in each st to last 2 hdc, (2 hdc) in next 2 hdc, turn—38 hdc.

Row 3: Rep row 2—42 hdc.

Row 4: Ch 2, (2 hdc) in next hdc, hdc in each st to last hdc, (2 hdc) in next hdc, turn—44 hdc.

Row 5: Ch 2, hdc in each hdc across, turn.

Row 6: Rep row 4—46 hdc.

Rows 7–9: Rep row 5.

Row 10: Rep row 4—48 hdc.

Rows 11–13: Rep row 5.

Row 14: Rep row 4—50 hdc.

Rows 15–32: Rep row 5.

Row 33: Ch 2, sk 1st hdc, hdc in each st to last 2 hdc, sk next hdc, hdc in last hdc, turn—48 hdc.

Row 34: Rep row 33—46 hdc.

Row 35: Rep row 33—44 hdc.

Row 36: Ch 2, [sk next st, hdc in next hdc] twice, hdc in each st to last 4 hdc, [sk next st, hdc in next hdc] twice, turn —40 hdc.

Row 37: Rep row 36—36 hdc.

Row 38: Rep row 36—32 hdc.

Row 39: Rep row 36 but do *not* turn—28 hdc.

Fasten off A.

Border

Join B. Work 1 rnd of sc evenly around entire edge of pieces, increasing (2 sc in one st) on outer curves and decreasing (skip sts) in dips and valleys where necessary so that border lies flat. Join with sl st at end of rnd and fasten off.

Snout

With A, ch 8.

Rnd 1: Hdc in 3rd ch from hook, hdc in next 4 hdc, (5 hdc) in last ch, working in opposite side of foundation ch, hdc in next 4 ch, (4 hdc) in last ch, join with sl st in 1st hdc, turn—18 hdc. Place marker for beg of rnd.

Rnd 2: Ch 2, (2 hdc) in next 4 hdc, hdc in next 4 hdc, (2 hdc) in next 5 hdc, hdc in next 4 hdc, (2 hdc) in last hdc, join with sl st in 1st hdc, turn—28 hdc.

Rnd 3: Ch 2, hdc in next 7 hdc, [(2 hdc) in next hdc, hdc in next hdc] 4 times, hdc in next 6 hdc, [(2 hdc) in next hdc, hdc in next hdc] 3 times, (2 hdc) in last hdc, join with sl st in 1st hdc, turn—36 hdc.

Rnd 4: Ch 2, hdc in next hdc, [(2 hdc) in next hdc, hdc in next 2 hdc] 4 times, hdc in next 3 hdc, [(2 hdc) in next hdc, hdc in next 2 hdc] 5 times, hdc in next 3 hdc, (2 hdc) in next hdc, hdc in last hdc, join with sl st in 1st hdc, turn—46 hdc.

Rnd 5: Ch 2, hdc in next 8 hdc, [(2 hdc) in next hdc, hdc in next 3 hdc] 4 times, 8 hdc, [(2 hdc) in next hdc, hdc in next 3 hdc] 3 times, (2 hdc) in next hdc, hdc in last hdc, join with sl st in 1st hdc, turn—54 sts.

Fasten off A. Join B.

Rnd 6 (RS): Ch 1, sc in next 2 sts, [(2 sc) in next st, sc in next 2 sts] 5 times, sc in next 12 sts, [(2 sc) in next st, sc in next sts] 5 times, sc in next 10 sts, join with sl st in 1st sc—64 sts.

Fasten off, leaving a tail 1 yd (1 m) long for sewing, and weave in the short end.

Nose

With B, ch 3 and sl st to 1st ch to form ring.

Rnd 1: Ch 2, work 12 dc in ring, join with sl st in 1st dc—12 dc.

Fasten off, leaving a tail 24" (61 cm) long for sewing, and weave in the short end.

Eye (make 2)

With B, ch 5.

Rnd 1: Dc in 3rd ch from hook, (6 dc) in last ch, working in opposite side of foundation ch, dc in next ch, (5 dc) in last ch join with sl st in 1st dc—14 dc.

Fasten off, leaving a tail 18" (45.5 cm) long for sewing later, and weave in short end.

Cap Base

With C, ch 9.

Row 1: Sc in 2nd ch from hook, sc in next 7 ch, turn—8 sc.

Rows 2–23: Ch 1, in BLO, sc in each sc across, turn.

Fasten off, leaving a tail 24" (60 cm) long for sewing later. Join B.

Rnd 1 (RS): Ch 1, working in both loops, sc in next 7 sc, (3 sc) in last st to turn corner, working along the sides of rows 1–23, work 22 sc evenly, (3 sc) in next st to turn corner, sc in next 6 sts, (3 sc) in last st to turn the corner, work 22 sc evenly along the opposite side of rows 1–23, (2 sc) in same st as first sc in rnd, join with sl st to 1st sc—68 sc.

Fasten off, leaving a tail 1yd (1 m) long for sewing, and weave in rem ends.

Cap Top

With D, ch 6.

Row 1: Sc in 2nd ch from hook, sc in next 4 ch, turn—5 sc.

Row 2: Ch 1, sc in each sc across, turn.

Row 3: Ch 1, (2 sc) in 1st sc, sc in next 4 sc—6 sc.

Row 4: Ch 1, sc in each sc across, turn.

Row 5: Ch 1, sc in next 5 sc, (2 sc) in last sc, turn—7 sc.

Row 6: Ch 1, sc in each sc across, turn.

Row 7: Ch 1, (2 sc) in 1st sc, sc in next 6 sc, turn—8 sc.

Row 8: Ch 1, sc in each sc across, turn.

Fasten off D. Join B.

Rnd 1 (RS): Ch 1, sc in next 7 sc, (3 sc) in last sc to turn corner, work 7 sc evenly along the side of rows 1–8, (2 sc) in next st for corner, sc in 3 sts of foundation ch, (2 sc) in last st to turn corner, work 7 sc evenly along the other side of rows 1–8, work (2 sc) in same st as 1st sc of rnd, join with sl st—33 sc.

Fasten off, leaving a tail 24" (61 cm) long for sewing, and weave in rem ends.

(continued)

Left Arm

With A, ch 8 (for top of arm).

Row 1: Hdc in 3rd ch from hook, 5 hdc in each ch across, turn —6 hdc.

Row 2: Ch 2, (2 hdc) in 1st hdc, hdc in next 4 hdc, leave last st unworked, turn.

Row 3: Ch 2, sk 1st hdc, hdc in next 4 hdc, (2 hdc) in last hdc, turn—6 hdc.

Rows 4–5: Rep rows 2–3.

Row 6: Ch 2, (2 hdc) in next 2 hdc, hdc in next 2 hdc, dc in next hdc, leave last st unworked, turn—7 sts.

Row 7: Ch 2, sk 1st st, dc in next st, hdc in next 3 sts, (2 hdc) in next 2 sts, turn—8 sts.

Row 8: Ch 2, (2 hdc) in 1st st, hdc in next 5 sts, dc in next st, leave last st unworked, turn—8 sts.

Row 9: Ch 2, sk 1st st, dc in next st, hdc in next 5 sts, (2 hdc) in last st—8 sts

Rows 10–11: Rep rows 8–9.

Row 12: Ch 2, (2 hdc) in next 2 sts, hdc in next 2 sts, dc in next 3 sts, leave last st unworked, turn—9 sts.

Row 13: Ch 2, sk 1st st, dc in next 3 sts, hdc in next 3 sts, (2 hdc) in next 2 sts, turn—10 sts.

Row 14: Ch 2, (2 hdc) in next 2 sts, hdc in next 4 sts, dc in next 3 sts, leave last st unworked, turn—11 sts.

Row 15: Ch 2, sk 1st st, dc in next 3 sts, hdc in next 5 sts, (2 hdc) in next 2 sts—12 sts.

Row 16: Ch 2, hdc in next 7 sts, dc in next 4 sts, leave last st unworked, turn—11 sts.

Row 17: Ch 2, sk 1st st, dc in next 8 sts, dc2tog, turn—9 sts.

Row 18: Ch 2, dc2tog, dc in next st, hdc in next 4 sts, dc in next 2 sts, turn—8 sts.

Row 19: Ch 2, sk 1st st, dc in next 2 sts, hdc in next 3 sts, sc2tog, do *not* turn—6 sts.

Fasten off A. Join B with RS facing.

Work border as for body and head, being sure that edge lies flat. Join with sl st and fasten off, leaving a tail 1 yd (1 m) long for sewing, and weave in rem ends.

Right Arm

Work as for left arm, working border with WS of arm facing.

Left Leg

With A, ch 8 (for bottom of foot).

Row 1: (2 hdc) in 3rd ch from hook, hdc in next 4 ch, (2 hdc) in last ch, turn—8 hdc.

Row 2: Ch 2, (2 hdc) in next 2 hdc, hdc in next 4 hdc, (2 hdc) in next 2 hdc, turn—12 hdc.

Rows 3–7: Ch 2, hdc in each st across, turn.

Row 8: Ch 2, sk 1st hdc, hdc in each st across, turn—11 hdc.

Row 9: Ch 2, (2 hdc) in 1st hdc, hdc in each st to last 2 hdc, sk 1 st, hdc in last st, turn—11 sts.

Rows 10–11: Rep rows 8–9—10 sts.

Row 12: Ch 2, sk 1st hdc, hdc in next 7 hdc, dc in next 2 hdc, turn—9 sts.

Row 13: Ch 2, (2 dc) in next st, dc in next st, hdc in next 5 sts, sk 1 st, hdc in next st, do *not* turn—9 sts.

Fasten off A. Join B with RS facing.

Work border as for body and head, being sure that edge lies flat. Join with sl st and fasten off, leaving a tail 1 yd (1 m) long for sewing, and weave in rem ends.

Right Leg

Work as for left leg, working border with WS of arm facing.

Bib Tie (make 2)

With E, ch 5.

Row 1: Hdc in 3rd ch from hook, hdc in next 2 ch, turn—3 hdc.

Row 2: Ch 2, hdc in next 3 hdc, turn.

Rep row 2 until tie measures 24" (61 cm) or desired length from beg.

Work 1 rnd of sl st around entire tie, join with sl st in 1st st. Fasten off, leaving a tail 24" (61 cm) long for sewing, and weave in the short end.

Waist Tie (make 2)

Work as for bib tie, making each tie 30" (76 cm) long or desired length from beg. Complete as for bib tie.

Assembly

Using photo as guide, place cap top on cap base and sew together. To keep the sts hidden, sew from the back of the pieces and pick up only a loop or two from top so that the sts won't show through on the front of the cap.

With RS facing, pin cap in place on head, overlapping 3–4 rnds. Use the long tail from cap base to sew cap base to head.

Pin nose to top of snout, using photo as guide, and sew down.

With B, using surface sl st or chain stitch embroidery, create a smile.

Pin snout and eyes to head as desired and sew down.

Sew arms and legs to body using photo as guide.

With WS facing, sew bib ties to top of head and side of cap base working through all layers of fabric.

Sew waist ties in the same manner, where head and body meet and the arms overlap.

To ensure that apron does not stretch, store folded, do not hang.

breakfast dishcloths

Rise 'n' shine! This cheery trio of breakfast-themed dishcloths will greet you every sun-up as you prep your favorite wake-me-up beverage and morning meal. Use cotton yarn for absorbency and heat resistance since you'll be putting these babies to work as trivets for warm plates, giant coasters for coffee mugs, and, of course, for wiping down dishes after a good rinse. To be honest, I think that the waffle, fried egg, and cup o' coffee cloths are so cute, they make me happy simply as kitchen decorations!

INGREDIENTS

(4) worsted weight

Red Heart Creme de la Creme, 100% Combed Cotton, 2.5 oz (70 g)/125 yds (114 m) per skein: 1 skein each #0307 Tan (A), #0331 Fudge Brown (B), #0205 Golden Yellow (C), #0001 White (D), and #0500 Aqua (E)

TOOLS

H/8 (5.00 mm) crochet hook
tapestry needle
stitch marker

WAFFLE DISHCLOTH

Gauge (for all)

16 sts x 19 rows in sc = 4" (10 cm).
Take time to check gauge.

Finished Size

Approx 7.5" (19 cm) x 7.5" (19 cm)

Special Stitches Used

FRONT POST DOUBLE CROCHET (FPDC)
Yo, insert hook from front to back and to front again around
the post of stitch on the previous row, yo, and draw up a loop,
complete as for a regular dc. Work the next st in next st of
previous row.

Waffle

With A, ch 32.

Row 1 (RS): Dc in 4th ch from hook, (counts as 2 dc), dc in next
28 ch, turn—30 dc.

Row 2: Ch 2 (counts dc throughout), sk 1st st, dc in next st,
[FPdc in next 2 dc, dc in next st] 9 times, dc in last dc, then
dc in ch-2 space, turn—30 dc.

Row 3: Ch 2, sk 1st st, [FPdc in next st, dc in next 2 sts] 9 times,
FPdc in last dc, then dc into ch-2 space, turn.

Rows 4-17: Rep rows 2–3 seven times more.

Row 18: Rep row 2.

With RS facing, work 1 rnd of dc evenly around the entire edge,
working 3 dc in each corner, join with sl st in first dc, ch 15
for hanging loop and sl st in same st.

Fasten off and weave in ends.

Syrup

With B, ch 3, join with sl st to form ring. Place marker for beg of
rnd.

Rnd 1: Ch 3, work 12 dc in ring, join with sl st in 1st dc—12 dc.

Rnd 2: Ch 7, dc in 4th ch from hook, dc in next 3, sl st in next
2 sts, [ch 9, dc in 4th ch from hook, dc next 6 ch, sl st in next
2 sts] twice, ch 6, dc in 4th ch from hook, dc in next 2 ch, sl
st in next 2 sts, ch 11, dc in 4th ch from hook, dc in next 7 ch,
sl st in next 2 sts, ch 6, dc in 4th ch from hook, dc in next 2
ch, sl st in next 2 sts. Fasten off, leaving a tail 1 yd (1 m) long
for sewing. Weave in other end.

Butter

With C, ch 3, join with sl st to form ring. Place marker for beg
of rnd.

Rnd 1: Ch 1, work 8 sc in ring, join with sl st in 1st sc—8 sc.

Rnd 2: Ch 2, (dc, hdc) in next st, [sc in next sc, (hdc, dc, hdc) in
next sc] 3 times, sc in next sc, hdc in next sc, join with sl st in
1st dc. Fasten off, leaving a tail 18" (45.5 cm) long for sewing.

Assembly

Using photo as guide and straight sts, sew butter to syrup and
syrup to waffle.

FRIED EGG DISHCLOTH

Finished Size

Approx 8.5" (21.5 cm) x 8" (20.5 cm)

Egg White

With D, ch 3, join with sl st to form ring. Place marker for beg of rnd.

Rnd 1: Ch 1, work 1 sc and 9 hdc in ring—10 sts. Do *not* join, rather work in a continuous spiral.

Rnd 2: (2 hdc) in each st around—20 hdc.

Rnd 3: [(2 hdc) in next hdc, hdc in next hdc] 10 times—30 sts.

Rnd 4: [(2 hdc) in next hdc, hdc in next 2 hdc] 10 times—40 sts.

Rnd 5: [(2 hdc) in next hdc, hdc in next 3 hdc] 10 times—50 sts.

Rnd 6: [(2 hdc) in next hdc, hdc in next 4 hdc] 10 times—60 sts.

Rnd 7: [(2 hdc) in next hdc, hdc in next 5 hdc] 10 times—70 sts.

Rnd 8: [(2 hdc) in next hdc, hdc in next 6 hdc] 10 times—80 sts.

Rnd 9: [(2 hdc) in next hdc, hdc in next 7 hdc] 9 times, (2 sc) in next hdc, sc in next 7 hdc, join with sl st in next st—90 sts.

Rnd 10: Sc in next 3 sts, hdc in next 2 sts, dc in next 2 sts, (2 htr) in next st, [tr in next 2 sts, (2 tr) in next st] twice, tr in next 2 sts, (2 htr) in next st, dc in next st, hdc in next st, sc in next 2 sts, [hdc in next st, (dc, htr) in next st, tr in next st, (2 tr) in next st, tr in next st, (htr, dc) in next st, hdc in next st, sc in next 2 sts] twice, hdc in next st, dc in next st, (2 htr) in next st, [tr in next 2 sts, (2 tr) in next st] twice, tr in next 2 sts, (2 htr) in next st, dc in next st, hdc in next 3 sts, sc in next 3 sts, hdc in next 2 sts, dc in next 2 sts, (2 htr) in next st, [tr in next 6 sts, (2 tr) in next st] twice, tr in next 6 sts, (2 htr) in next st, dc in next 2 sts, hdc in next 2 sts, sc in next st, join with sl st in next st, ch 15 for hanging loop and join in same st. Fasten off and weave in ends.

Egg Yolk

With C work rnds 1–4 as for egg white.

Rnd 5: Sc in next st, join with sl st in next st.

Fasten off, leaving a tail 24" (61 cm) for sewing later, and weave in other end.

Assembly

Using photo as guide and straight sts, sew egg yolk to top of egg white.

COFFEE CUP DISHCLOTH

Finished size

Approx 7.5" (19 cm) x 7.5" (19 cm), excluding handle

Top of Cup

With B, ch 21, loosely.

Rnd 1: Sc in 2nd ch from hook, sc next 18 ch, (3 sc) in last ch, working in opposite side of foundation ch, sc in next 18 ch, (2 sc) in last ch, join with sl st in 1st sc, turn—42 sc.

Rnd 2: Ch 1, (2 sc) in next 2 sc, sc in next 18 sc, (2 sc) in next 3 sc, sc in next 18 sc, (2 sc) in next sc, join with sl st in 1st sc, turn—48 sc.

Rnd 3: Ch 1, (2 sc), sc in next 19 sc, [(2 sc) in next sc, sc in next sc] twice, (2 sc) in next sc, sc in next 19 sc, [(2 sc) in next sc, sc in next sc] twice join with sl st in 1st sc, turn—54 sc.

Rnd 4: Ch 1, (2 sc in next sc), sc in next 2 sc, (2 sc) in next sc, sc in next 20 sc, [(2 sc) in next sc, sc in next 2 sc] twice, (2 sc) in next sc, sc in next 20 sc, (2 sc) in next, sc in next 2 sc, join with sl st in 1st sc, turn—60 sc.

Fasten off B. Join E.

Rnd 5: Ch 1, (2 sc) in next sc, sc in next 21 sc, [(2 sc) in next sc, sc in next 3 sc] twice, (2 sc) in next sc, sc in next 21 sc, [(2 sc) in next sc, sc in next 3 sc] twice, join with sl st in 1st sc, turn—66 sc.

Rnd 6: Ch 1, (2 sc) in next sc, sc in next 4 sc, (2 sc) in next sc, sc in next 22 sc, [(2 sc) in next sc, sc in next 4 sc] twice, (2 sc) in next sc, sc in next 22 sc, (2 sc) in next sc, sc in next 4 sc, join with sl st in 1st sc, turn—72 sc.

Middle of Cup

(worked in rows)

Row 1 (WS): Ch 1, sk the last sl st from rnd 6, sl st in next sc, sc in next sc, (2 sc) in next sc, sc in next 24 sc, (2 sc) in next sc, sc in next sc, sl st in next st, turn—32 sts.

Rows 2–9: Ch 1, sk 1st st, sl st in next st, sc in next, (2 sc) in next st, sc in next 24 sts, (2 sc) in next st, sc in next st, sk 1 st, sl st in last st, turn.

Bottom of Cup

Note: Work edge sts loosely to prevent curling.

Row 10: Ch 1, sk 1st st, sl st in next st, sc2tog, (2 sc) in next sc, sc in next 22 sc, (2 sc) in next sc, sc2tog, sk 1 st, sl st in next st, turn—30 sc.

Row 11: Ch 1, sk 1st st, sl st in next st, sc in next sc, (2 sc) in next sc, sc in next 22 sc, (2 sc) in next sc, sc in next sc, sk 1 st, sl st in next st, turn.

Row 12: Ch 1, sk 1st st, sl st in next st, sc2tog, (2 sc) in next sc, sc in next 20 sc, (2 sc) in next sc, sc2tog, sk 1 st, sl st in next st, turn—28 sc.

Row 13: Ch 1, sk 1st st, sl st in next st, sc in next sc, (2 sc) in next sc, sc in next 20 sc, (2 sc) in next sc, sc in next sc, sk 1 st, sl st in next st, turn.

Row 14: Ch 1, sk 1st st, sl st in next st, sc2tog, (2 sc) in next sc, sc in next 18 sc, (2 sc) in next sc, sc2tog, sk 1 st, sl st in next st, turn—26 sc.

Row 15: Ch 1, sk 1st st, sl st in next st, sc in next sc, (2 sc) in next sc, sc in next 18 sc, (2 sc) in next sc, sc in next sc, sk 1 st, sl st in next st, turn.

Row 16: Ch 1, sk 1st st, sl st in next st, sc2tog, (2 sc) in next sc, sc in next 16 sc, (2 sc) in next sc, sc2tog, sk 1 st, sl st in next st, turn—24 sc.

Row 17: Ch 1, sk 1st st, sl st in next st, sc in next sc, (2 sc) in next sc, sc in next 16 sc, (2 sc) in next sc, sc in next sc, sk 1 st, sl st in next st, turn.

Row 18: Ch 1, sk 1st st, sl st in next st, sc2tog, (2 sc) in next sc, sc in next 14 sc, (2 sc) in next sc, sc2tog, sk 1 st, sl st in next st, turn—22 sts.

Row 19: Ch 1, sk 1st st, sl st in next st, sc in next sc, (2 sc) in next sc, sc in next 14 sc, (2 sc), sc in next sc, sk 1 st, sl st in next st.

Row 20: Ch 1, sk 1st st, sl st in next st, sc2tog, (2 sc) in next sc, sc in next 12 sc, (2 sc) in next sc, sc2tog, sk 1 st, sl st in next st, turn—20 sc.

Row 21: Ch 1, sk 1st st, sl st in next st, sc in next sc, (2 sc) in next sc, sc in next 12 sc, (2 sc) in next sc, sc in next sc, sk 1 st, sl st in next st, turn.

Row 22: Ch 1, sk 1st st, sl st in next st, sc2tog, (2 sc) in next sc, sc in next 10 sc, (2 sc) in next, sc2tog, sk 1 st, sl st in next st, turn—18 sc.

Fasten off and weave in all ends.

Assembly

HANGING LOOP
Join E to top center of coffee cup, ch 15 and sl st in same st as joining. Fasten off and weave in ends.

COFFEE SWIRL
With A, add swirl to coffee, using surface slip stitch or embroidered chain st.

CUP EMBELLISHMENTS
With D, embellish the coffee cup, using surface slip stitch or embroidered chain st.

Cup Handle

With RS of coffee cup facing you, join E to edge of row 12 of coffee cup, ch 18, sl st in the first free st on rnd 6 and sl st in the next st, turn—18 sts.

Row 1: Ch 1, work 24 sc evenly in the ch-18 space, join with sl st in the edge of row 13, sl st in edge of row 14, turn—24 sc.

Row 2: Ch 1, sc in next 4 sc, (2 sc) in next sc, sc in next 12 sc, (2 sc) in next sc, sc in next 4 sc, join with sl st to next st in rnd 6, sl st in next st, turn.

Row 3: Ch 1, sc in next 3 sc, (2 sc) in next, sc in next 16 sc, (2 sc) in next sc, 3 sc join with sl st in edge of row 15. Fasten off and weave in ends.

cherry pie seat cushion

My dining chairs are just plain ol' wooden ones that we painted different colors. While I've gone through various store-bought seat cushions, I figured it was *pie time* to DIY my own. This comfy cozy cherry pie seat cushion pairs perfectly with my red-and-white checkered table cloth, and you and your dinner guests are guaranteed to love their country-cute charm! You will go through quite a bit of yarn while crocheting the biggest pie I have ever seen, but if you are familiar already with working in the round, this is a really easy pattern to modify and fit a range of cushion sizes.

INGREDIENTS

(4) worsted weight

Lion Brand Vanna's Choice, 100% Premium Acrylic, 3.5 oz (100 g)/170 yds (156 m) per skein: 4 skeins #860-130 Honey (A), 2 skeins #860-113 Scarlet (B)

Foam cushion 17" (43 cm) diameter x 2" (5 cm) deep

TOOLS

I/9 (5.5 mm) crochet hook
tapestry needle
stitch marker
straight pins

DIRECTIONS

Gauge

14 sts x 17 rows in sc = 4" (10 cm).
Take time to check gauge.

Finished Size

17" (43 cm) diameter, excluding ruffle

Special Stitches Used

BOBBLE

Yo, insert hook into desired stitch, yo and draw up a loop, yo, draw through 2 loops on hook [yo, insert hook into same stitch, yo and draw up a loop, yo, draw through 2 loops on hook] twice, yo and draw through all 4 loops on hook. Bobble is complete and pops out on the back of your work.

DOUBLE TREBLE CROCHET (DTR)

[Yo] 3 times, insert hook into desired stitch, yo and draw up a loop, [yo, draw through 2 loops on hook] 4 times.

Cherry Filling

With B, ch 3, join with sl st to form ring. Place marker for beg of rnd.

Rnd 1: Ch 1, 6 sc into ring, join with sl st to 1st sc—6 sts.

Rnd 2: Ch 1, [sc in next st, bobble in next st] 6 times, join with sl st to 1st sc—12 sts.

Rnd 3: Ch 1, [(2 sc) in next st] 12 times, join with sl st to 1st sc—24 sts.

Rnd 4: Ch 1, [sc in next 2 sts, bobble in next st] 8 times, join with sl st to 1st sc.

Rnd 5: Ch 1, [(2 sc) in next st, sc in next st] 12 times, join with sl st to 1st sc—36 sts.

Rnd 6: Ch 1, [sc in next 2 sts, bobble in next st] 12 times, join with sl st to 1st sc.

Rnd 7: Ch 1, [(2 sc) in next st, sc in next 2 sts] 12 times, join with sl st to 1st sc—48 sts.

Rnd 8: Ch 1, [sc in next 2 sts, bobble in next st] 16 times, join with sl st to 1st sc.

Rnd 9: Ch 1, [(2 sc) in next st, sc in next 3 sts] 12 times, join with sl st to 1st sc—60 sts.

Rnd 10: Ch 1, [sc in next 2 sts, bobble in next] 20 times, join with sl st to 1st sc.

Rnd 11: Ch 1, [(2 sc) in next st, sc in next 4 sts] 12 times, join with sl st to 1st sc—72 sts.

Rnd 12: Ch 1, [sc in next 2 sts, bobble in next st] 24 times, join with sl st to 1st sc.

Rnd 13: Ch 1, [(2 sc) in next st, sc in next 5 sts] 12 times, join with sl st to 1st sc—84 sts.

Rnd 14: Ch 1, [sc in next 2 sts, bobble in next st] 28 times, join with sl st to 1st sc.

Rnd 15: Ch 1, [(2 sc) in next st, sc in next 6 sts] 12 times, join with sl st to 1st sc—96 sts.

Rnd 16: Ch 1, [sc in next 2 sts, bobble in next st] 32 times, join with sl st to 1st sc.

Rnd 17: Ch 1, [(2 sc) in next st, sc in next 7 sts] 12 times, join with sl st to 1st sc—108 sts.

Rnd 18: Ch 1, [sc in next 2 sts, bobble in next st] 36 times, join with sl st to 1st sc.

Rnd 19: Ch 1, [(2 sc) in next st, sc in next 8 sts] 12 times, join with sl st to 1st sc—120 sts.

Rnd 20: Ch 1, [sc in next 2 sts, bobble in next st] 40 times, join with sl st to 1st sc.

Rnd 21: Ch 1, [(2 sc) in next st, sc in next 9 sts] 12 times, join with sl st to 1st sc—132 sts.

Rnd 22: Ch 1, [sc in next 2 sts, bobble in next st] 44 times, join with sl st to 1st sc.

Rnd 23: Ch 1, [(2 sc) in next st, sc in next 10 sts] 12 times, join with sl st to 1st sc—144 sts.

Rnd 24: Ch 1, [sc in next 2 sts, bobble in next st] 48 times, join with sl st to 1st sc.

Rnd 25: Ch 1, [(2 sc) in next st, sc in next 11 sts] 12 times, join with sl st to 1st sc—156 sts.

Rnd 26: Ch 1, [sc in next 2 sts, bobble in next st] 52 times, join with sl st to 1st sc.

Rnd 27: Ch 1, [(2 sc) in next st, sc in next 12 sts] 12 times, join with sl st to 1st sc—168 sts.

Rnd 28: Ch 1, [sc in next 2 sts, bobble in next st] 56 times, join with sl st to 1st sc.

Rnd 29: Ch 1, [(2 sc) in next st, sc in next 27 sts] 6 times, join with sl st to 1st sc—174 sts.

Fasten off and weave in ends.

(continued)

Piecrust

With A, ch 3, join with sl st to form ring. Place marker for beg of rnd.

Rnd 1: Ch 1, work 6 sc in ring—6 sc. Do *not* join.
Rnd 2: Ch 1, [(2 sc) in next sc] 6 times—12 sc.
Rnd 3: Ch 1, [(2 sc) in next sc] 12 times—24 sc.
Rnd 4: Ch 1, sc in each sc around.
Rnd 5: Ch 1, [(2 sc) in next sc, sc in next sc] 12 times—36 sts.
Rnd 6: Ch 1, sc in each sc around
Rnd 7: Ch 1, [(2 sc) in next sc, sc in next 2 sc] 12 times—48 sc.
Rnd 8: Ch 1, sc in each sc around.
Rnd 9: Ch 1, [(2 sc) in next sc, sc in next 3 sc] 12 times—60 sc.
Rnd 10: Ch 1, sc in each sc around.
Rnd 11: Ch 1, [(2 sc) in next sc, sc in next 4 sc] 12 times—72 sc.
Rnd 12: Ch 1, sc in each sc around.
Rnd 13: Ch 1, [(2 sc) in next sc, sc in next 5 sc] 12 times—84 sc.
Rnd 14: Ch 1, sc in each sc around.
Rnd 15: Ch 1, [(2 sc) in next sc, sc in next 6 sc] 12 times—96 sc.
Rnd 16: Ch 1, sc in each sc around.
Rnd 17: Ch 1, [(2 sc) in next sc, sc in next 7 sc] 12 times—108 sc.
Rnd 18: Ch 1, sc in each sc around.
Rnd 19: Ch 1, [(2 sc) in next sc, sc in next 8 sc] 12 times—120 sc.
Rnd 20: Ch 1, sc in each sc around.
Rnd 21: Ch 1, [(2 sc) in next sc, sc in next 9 sc] 12 times—132 sc.
Rnd 22: Ch 1, sc in each sc around.
Rnd 23: Ch 1, [(2 sc) in next sc, sc in next 10 sc] 12 times—144 sc.
Rnd 24: Ch 1, sc in each sc around.
Rnd 25: Ch 1, [(2 sc) in next sc, sc in next 11 sc] 12 times—156 sc.
Rnd 26: Ch 1, sc in each sc around.
Rnd 27: Ch 1, [(2 sc) in next sc, sc in next 12 sc] 12 times—168 sc.
Rnd 28: Ch 1, sc in each sc around.
Rnd 29: Ch 1, [(2 sc) in next sc, sc in next 13 sc] 12 times—180 sc.
Rnd 30: Ch 1, sc in each sc around, join with sl st in 1st sc.

Side of Pie

Rnd 31: Ch 1, working in BLO, sc in each sc around. Do *not* join. Place marker for beg of rnd.
Rnd 32: Ch 1, working in both loops, sc in each sc around, turn.
Rep this rnd 6 times more, or until the side of pie is the same depth as the foam cushion. Join with sl st at end of final rnd. Turn.

Ruffled Edge

Edge rnd: Ch 4, *(Note: RS of this rnd faces the inside of pie)* (3 dtr) in each st around, join with sl st in first dtr.
Fasten off, leaving a tail 1 yd (1 m) long for sewing, and weave in rem ends.

Strip A (Make 4)

With A, ch 56 loosely.
Row 1: Hdc in 3rd ch from hook, hdc in each ch across, turn —54 hdc.
Rows 2–3: Ch 2, hdc in each hdc across.
Fasten off, leaving a tail 1 yd (1 m) long for sewing, and weave in other end.

Strip B (make 4)

With A, ch 48 loosely. Complete as for strip A.

Strip C (make 4)

With A, ch 38 loosely.
Row 1: Hdc in 3rd ch from hook, hdc in each ch across, turn —36 hdc.
Row 2: Ch 2, (2 hdc) in first hdc, 34 hdc, (2 hdc) in last hdc, turn—38 hdc.
Row 3: Ch 2, hdc in each hdc across.
Fasten off, leaving a tail 1 yd (1 m) long for sewing, and weave in other end.

Tie Strings (make 2)

With A, make a loose ch approx 21" (53.5 cm) long.
Row 1: Sl st in 2nd ch from hook and in each ch across, being sure to work through both loops of each ch. Fasten off and weave in ends.

Assembly

Place cushion on top of piecrust, being sure that the RS of pie crust is facing out. Place cherry filling on top of cushion, being sure the bobbles are showing. Pin the pieces together all the way around. Weave the long tail from the piecrust down to the base of the st. Sew edge of cherry filling to bottom of the dtrs on the pie crust (**Photo 1**), using 1 yd (1 m) of yarn at a time. Note that the crust and filling have different numbers of sts, so use a zig-zag st to ease them together evenly.

LATTICE TOP

Place 2 A strips across the center of the cherry filling, place 1 B strip on each side of the A strips, place 1 C strip outside each B strip. Place the C strips so that the angled edges match the shape of the pie edge, one with the RS facing and one with the WS facing. Arrange the rest of the placed strips to alternate which side is facing, place them 1" (2.5 cm) apart. Pin ends of strips to the pie edge. (**Photo 2**)

Arrange the remaining 6 strips across the placed strips in the same way. Weave the strips over and under the placed strips and pin in place.

Sew the long edges of each strip to the cherry filling. Sew the short edges of each strip to the piecrust at the base of the dtrs.

TIES

Place cushion on the chair and pin tie strings in place. Adjust as necessary. Sew the tie strings to the cushion, using photo as guide. (**Photo 3**).

living & lounging

My living room is my favorite place to relax and get cozy, and crocheted accents are the perfect medium for maximizing your comfort. The patterns in this chapter will range from a delicate sprinkle of sugar—with a nostalgic cookie garland—up to a big splash of color—with a bold candy blanket. Ever dreamed of having a giant donut to sit on?

Donut dream any longer!

frosted animal cookie garland

When I was little, a bag of pink and white animal cookies was such a cute and exciting treat. Every time I see these cookies now, they make me smile! Hang up this sweetly nostalgic garland for someone's special party or for sprinkling sugar over any room any day. You can also use this pattern to make adorable brooches. Just use a lighter weight yarn and a smaller hook size, crochet two of whichever animal you like, leave off the bordering round of single crochet, and sew the two shapes together like a tiny pillow with some polyester stuffing inside. If pink and white isn't your color palette, you can use a light tan yarn to make yourself some animal crackers. Get wild!

INGREDIENTS

(4) worsted weight

Red Heart With Love, 100% Acrylic, 7 oz (198 g)/370 yds
(338 m) per skein: 1 skein each #E400-1704 Bubble Gum
(A), and #E400-1001 White (B)

Note: Each animal requires approx 15 yds (14 m) of yarn

TOOLS

I/9 (5.5 mm) crochet hook
K/10.5 (6.50 mm) crochet hook
tapestry needle
5-mm mini pompoms in rainbow colors
fabric glue

Gauge

13 sts x 15 rows in sc with larger hook = 4" (10 cm).
Take time to check gauge.

Finished Size

7-animal garland measures approx 57" (144.5 cm) long

Notes:
1. *Animals are worked in rows from nose to tail, so that rows run vertically, up and down each animal.*
2. *Be sure that sl sts are worked loosely, since sts may be worked in them later.*
3. *The colors, combinations, and number of animals in your garland are entirely up to you! 7 animals are used in the sample.*

RHINO

Finished Size

Approx 5" (12.5 cm) x 3.5" (9 cm)

Rhino (Make 1 Each in A and B)

With larger hook, ch 5.
Row 1: Sc in 2nd ch from hook, sc in next 3 sc, turn—4 sc.
Row 2: Ch 1, (2 sc) in next sc, sc in next 2 sc, (2 sc) in next sc, turn—6 sc.
Row 3: Ch 3, sc in 2nd and 3rd ch from hook, sc in 5 sc, (2 sc) in next sc, turn—9 sc.
Row 4: Ch 1, sc in next 9 sc, turn.
Row 5: Ch 1, sl st in next 2 sc, sc in next 7 sc, turn.
Row 6: Ch 1, sk 1 st, sc in next 4 sc, sc2tog, turn, leaving rem sts unworked—5 sc.

Row 7: Ch 1, sc in next 5 sc, turn.
Row 8: Ch 1, (2 sc) in next sc, sc in next 3 sc, (2 sc) in next sc, turn—7 sc.
Row 9: Ch 3, sc in 2nd and 3rd ch from hook, sc in next 7 sc, turn—9 sc.
Row 10: Ch 1, sc in 9 sc, turn.
Row 11: Ch 1, sl st in next 2 sts, sc in next 5 sc, sc2tog, turn—6 sc.
Row 12: Ch 1, sk 1st st, sc in next 5 sc, turn, leaving rem sts unworked—5 sc.
Row 13: Ch 1, (2 sc) in next sc, sc in next 4 sc, turn—6 sc.
Row 14: Ch 1, sk 1st st, sl st in next sc, sc in next 4 sc, turn—4 sc.
Row 15: Ch 1, sc in next 4 sc, turn.
Row 16: Ch 1, sc in next 2 sc, sc2tog, turn—3 sc.
Border rnd: Ch 1, work 1 rnd of sc evenly around the entire piece, being sure that border lies flat, join with sl st to 1st sc. (**Photo 1**) Fasten off and weave in ends.

(continued)

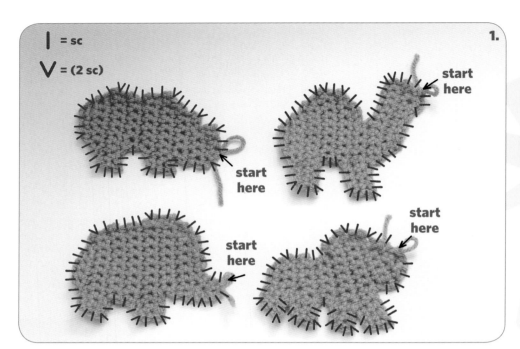

I = sc

V = (2 sc)

1.

start here

start here

start here

start here

When crocheting the border round for each animal, decrease (skip stitches) on inside corners and increase (2 sc in one st) on outside curves to keep the border lying flat.

CAMEL

Finished Size
Approx 5.25" (13.5 cm) x 4.5" (11.5 cm)

Camel (Make 1 Each in A and B)

With larger hook, ch 5.

Row 1: Sc in 2nd ch from hook, sc in next 4 sc, turn—4 sc.

Row 2: Ch 1, (2 sc) in next sc, sc in next 2 sc, (2 sc) in next sc, turn—6 sc.

Row 3: Ch 4, sc in 2nd ch from hook, sc in rem 2 ch, tsc in next 5 sc, (2 sc) in next sc, turn—10 sc.

Row 4: Ch 1, (2 sc) in next sc, sc in next 9 sc, turn—11 sc.

Row 5: Ch 1, sl st in next 4 sc, sc in next 6 sc, (2 sc) in next sc, turn—8 sc.

Row 6: Ch 1, sc in next 8 sc, turn—8 sc.

Row 7: Ch 1, sc in next 8 sc, turn.

Row 8: Ch 1, sk 1 st, sc in next 7 sc, turn—7 sc.

Row 9: Ch 5, sc in 2nd ch from hook, sc in rem 4 ch, sc in next 5 sc, sc2tog, turn—10 sc.

Row 10: Ch 1, sk 1st st, sl st in next sc, sc in next 8 sc, turn—9 sc.

Row 11: Ch 1, sl st in next 3 sts, sc in next 5 sc, turn, leaving rem st unworked—8 sts.

Row 12: Ch 7, sc in 2nd ch from hook, sc in rem 6 ch, sc in next 3 sc, sc2tog, turn, leaving rem sts unworked—10 sc.

Row 13: Ch 1, sk 1st st, sc in next 9 sc, turn—9 sc.

Row 14: Ch 1, sk 1st st, sc in next 6 sc, sc2tog, turn—7 sc.

Row 15: Ch 1, sk 1st st, sl st in next 4 sc, (sl st, ch 1, sc) in next sc, sc in next sc.

Border rnd: Ch 1, work 1 rnd of sc evenly around the entire piece, being sure that border lies flat, join with sl st to 1st sc. **(Photo 1)** Fasten off and weave in ends.

ELEPHANT

Finished Size
Approx 5.25" (13.5 cm) x 4" (10 cm)

Elephant (Make 2 in A)

With larger hook, ch 5.

Row 1: Sc in 2nd ch from hook, sc in next 3 ch, turn—4 sc.

Row 2: Ch 4, sc in 2nd ch from hook, sc in 2 rem ch, sc in next 3 sc, (3 sc) in next sc, turn—9 sc.

Row 3: Ch 1, (2 sc) in next sc, sc in next 8 sc, turn—10 sc.

Row 4: Ch 1, sc in each sc across, turn.

Row 5: Ch 1, sc in next 8 sc, turn, leaving rem sts unworked —8 sc.

Rows 6–7: Ch 1, sc in each sc across, turn.

Row 8: Ch 3, sc in 2nd and 3rd ch from hook, sc in next 8 sc, turn—10 sc.

Row 9: Ch 2, sc in 2nd ch from hook, sc in next 10 sc, turn—11 sc.

Row 10: Ch 1, sc in each sc across, turn.

Row 11: Ch 1, sc in next 8 sc, turn, leaving rem sts unworked —8 sc.

Row 12: Ch 1, (2 sc) in next sc, sc in next 7 sc, turn—9 sc.

Row 13: Ch 1, sk 1st st, sc2tog, sc in next 6 sc, turn—7 sc.

Row 14: Ch 5, sk 1st ch, [sc2tog] 2 times in ch (to curve trunk), sk next st, sc in next 5 sc, sl st in next sc, turn—8 sts.

Row 15: Ch 1, sk 1st st, sl st in next st, sc in next 2 sc, sl st in next st, sc in next 3 sts, turn—7 sts.

Border rnd: Ch 1, work 1 rnd of sc evenly around the entire piece, being sure that border lies flat, join with sl st to 1st sc. Fasten off and weave in ends.

LION

Finished Size
Approx 4.5" (11.5 cm) x 4" (10cm)

Lion (Make 1 in B)
With larger hook, ch 6.

Row 1: Sc in 2nd ch from hook, sc in next 3 ch, (2 sc) in last ch, turn—6 sc.

Row 2: Ch 1, sc in next 6 sc, turn.

Row 3: Ch 1, sl st in next 3 sc (bottom of 1st leg), ch 4, turn, sc in 2nd ch from hook, sc in rem 2 ch, sc in same st as 1st sl st, (2nd leg) sc in next 3 sc, turn—7 sts. **(Photo 2)**

Row 4: Ch 1, sc in each st across, turn.

Row 5: Ch 1, sl st in next 2 sts, (sl st, ch 1, sc) in next sc, sc in next 2 sc, sc2tog, turn—6 sts.

Row 6: Ch 1, sc in next 4 sc, turn, leaving rem sts unworked —4 sc.

Row 7: Ch 4, sc in 2nd ch from hook, sc in rem 3 ch, sc in next 3 sc, (2 sc) in next sc, turn—8 sc.

Row 8: Ch 1, (3 sc) in next sc, sc in next 7 sc, turn—10 sc.

Row 9: Ch 1, sl st in next 3 sc (bottom of 3rd leg), ch 4, turn, sc in 2nd ch from hook, sc in rem 2 ch, sc in same st as 1st sl st (4th leg) sc in next 7 sc, turn—11 sts.

Row 10: Ch 1, sc in each sc across.

2.

Row 11: Ch 1, sl st in next 4 sc, (sl st, ch 1, sc) in next st, sc in next 6 sc, turn—7 sc.

Row 12: Ch 1, sk 1st st, sc2tog, sc in next 3 sc, (2 sc) in next st, turn—6 sc.

Row 13: Ch 1, sc in next 4 sc, sc2tog, turn—5 sc.

Row 14: Ch 1, sk 1st st, sc2tog, sc in next 2 sc, turn—3 sc.

Row 15: Ch 1, sk 1 st, sc in next sc, sl st in next st.

Border rnd: Ch 1, work 1 rnd of sc evenly around the entire piece, being sure that border lies flat, join with sl st to 1st sc. **(Photo 1)** Fasten off and weave in ends.

ASSEMBLY

Place animals in desired order and add them to the garland in reverse order. Choose 2 points along the top edge of each animal to attach to the garland.

With smaller hook and B, ch 10 and sl st to form a hanging loop, ch 25, *sc in 1st point of first animal, work as many ch as needed to reach the 2nd point of the animal before attaching with sc in the 2nd point, ch 20; rep from * until all animals have been joined to the garland, ch 35, sl st to 10th ch from hook for hanging loop. Fasten off and weave in ends.

With fabric glue, add mini pompoms as desired for sprinkles.

banana split throw pillow

The banana split throw pillow is the absolute epitome of living à la mode! Three yummy scoops of ice cream, each topped with hot fudge, whipped cream, and a cherry, sit deliciously atop a perfect banana. You'll get to practice working in the round for the components in this project before sewing them all together. There's a lot of opportunity here to change up a variety of yarn colors and ice cream flavors, as well as your favorite sundae sauces, from hot fudge to caramel to strawberry!

INGREDIENTS

(4) worsted weight

Red Heart Super Saver Economy, 100% Acrylic, 7 oz (198 g)/364 yds (333 m) per skein: 2 skeins each #E300-235 Lemon (A), 1 skein each #E300-313 Aran (B), #E300-373 Petal Pink (D), #E300-365 Coffee (E), #E300-311 White (F), and #E300-319 Cherry Red (G)

Red Heart Classic, 100% Acrylic, 3.5 oz (100 g)/190 yds (174 m) per skein: 1 skein #E267-681 Mist Green (C)

5-mm mini pompoms in rainbow colors for sprinkles

TOOLS

H/8 (5.00 mm) crochet hook
32 oz (900 g) bag of polyester stuffing
tapestry needle
stitch marker
fabric glue

DIRECTIONS

Gauge

15 sts x 18 rows in sc = 4" (10 cm).
Take time to check gauge.

Finished Size

Length of Banana: Approx 35" (89 cm)
Height to Top of Center Cherry: Approx 15" (38 cm)

Banana

With A, ch 3, join with sl st to form ring. Place marker for beg of rnd.

Rnd 1: Ch 2, work 10 dc in ring, join with sl st in 1st dc, turn —10 dc.

Rnd 2: Ch 2, (2 dc) in each st around, join with sl st in 1st dc, turn—20 sts.

Rnd 3: Ch 2, [(2 dc) in next dc, dc in next dc] 10 times, join with sl st in 1st dc, turn—30 dc.

Rnd 4: Ch 2, [(2 dc) in next dc, dc in next 5 dc] 5 times, join with sl st in 1st dc, turn—35 dc.

Rnd 5: Ch 2, [(2 dc) in next dc, dc in next 6 dc] 5 times, join with sl st in 1st dc, turn—40 dc.

Rnd 6: Ch 2, [(2 dc) in next dc, dc in next 7 dc] 5 times, join with sl st in 1st dc, turn—45 dc.

Rnd 7: Ch 2, [(2 dc) in next dc, dc in next 8 dc] 5 times, join with sl st in 1st dc, turn—50 dc.

Rnd 8: Ch 2, [(2 dc) in next dc, dc in next 9 dc] 5 times, join with sl st in 1st dc, turn—55 dc.

Rnd 9: Ch 2, [(2 dc) in next dc, dc in next 10 dc] 5 times, join with sl st in 1st dc, turn—60 dc.

Rnds 10-12: Ch 2, dc in each dc around, join with sl st in 1st dc, turn.

Rnd 13: Ch 2, dc in next 20 dc, hdc in next 20 dc, dc in next 20 dc, join with sl st in 1st dc, turn.

Rnd 14: Ch 2, dc in each st around, join with sl st in 1st dc, turn.

Rnds 15-66: Rep rnds 13 and 14. Piece measures approx 31" (78.5 cm).

Rnds 67-68: Rep rnd 14.

Shape end

Note: Stuff banana before beginning to shape.
Cont to stuff as you go.

Rnd 69: Ch 2, [dc2tog, dc in next 10 dc] 5 times, join with sl st in 1st dc, turn—55 dc.

Rnd 70: Ch 2, [dc2tog, dc in next 9 dc] 5 times, join with sl st in 1st dc, turn—50 dc.

Rnd 71: Ch 2, [dc2tog, dc in next 8 dc] 5 times, join with sl st in 1st dc, turn—45 dc.

Rnd 72: Ch 2, [dc2tog, dc in next 7 dc] 5 times, join with sl st in 1st dc, turn—40 dc.

Rnd 73: Ch 2, [dc2tog, dc in next 6 dc] 5 times, join with sl st in 1st dc, turn—35 dc.

Rnd 74: Ch 2, [dc2tog, dc in next 5 dc] 5 times, join with sl st in 1st dc, turn—30 dc.

Rnd 75: Ch 2, [dc2tog, dc in next dc] 10 times, join with sl st in 1st dc, turn—20 dc.

Rnd 76: Ch 2, [dc2tog] 10 times, join with sl st in 1st dc, turn—10 dc.

Fasten off, leaving a long tail. Thread tail through the outside loops of the rem 10 sts and pull to close. Tie off and weave in ends. The seam where rnds are joined runs under the banana, and the banana ends curve upward.

49

(continued)

Center Ice Cream Scoop

Note: RS shows on outside of scoop.

With B, ch 3, join with sl st to form ring. Place marker for beg of rnd.

Rnd 1: Work sc, hdc, 10 dc in ring—12 sts. Do *not* join, rather work in a continuous spiral.

Rnd 2: (2 dc) in each st—24 dc.

Rnd 3: [(2 dc) in next dc, dc in next dc] 12 times—36 dc.

Rnd 4: [(2 dc) in next dc, dc in next 3 dc] 9 times—45 dc.

Rnd 5: [(2 dc) in next dc, dc in next 4 dc] 9 times—54 dc.

Rnd 6: [(2 dc) in next dc, dc in next 5 dc] 9 times—63 dc.

Rnd 7: [(2 dc) in next dc, dc in next 6 dc] 9 times—72 dc.

Rnd 8: [(2 dc) in next dc, dc in next 11 dc] 6 times—78 dc.

Rnd 9–16: Dc in each dc.

Rnd 17: Dc in next 68 dc, hdc in next 5 dc, sc in next 5 dc, join with sl st in next st.

Ruffle rnd: Ch 1, work in FLO as follows: [sl st in next 10 sts, (3 tr) in next 29 sts,] Fasten off, leaving a tail 1 yd (1 m) long for sewing.

Side Ice Cream Scoop (make 1 in each C and D)

Work as for center ice cream scoop through rnd 17—78 dc.

Ruffle rnd: Ch 1, work in FLO as follows: sl st in next 10 sts, (3 tr) in next 68 sts, join with sl st to next st.

Fasten off, leaving a tail 1 yd (1 m) long for sewing.

Hot Fudge Sauce (make 3)

SPECIAL MOTIFS

Short Drip: Ch 12, hdc in 3rd ch from hook, hdc in next 9 ch, sk next 2 sts of previous rnd, join with sl st.

Long Drip: Ch 14, hdc in 3rd ch from hook, hdc in next 11 ch, sk next 2 sts of previous rnd, join with sl st.

Curve: Sc in next st, dc in next st, (3 htr) in next st, dc in next st, sc in next st.

HOT FUDGE SAUCE

With E, ch 3, join with sl st to form ring. Place marker for beg of rnd.

Work rnds 1–7 as for center ice cream scoop. At end of rnd 7, work hdc in next 2 sts, sc in next 2 sts, join with sl st to round off the circle—72 sts.

Rnd 8: Work special motifs as follows: Short drip, 2 curves, short drip, long drip, curve, short drip, curve, long drip, short drip, 2 curves, long drip, curve, short drip, long drip, 2 curves, join with sl st in next st.

Fasten off, leaving a tail 2 yds (2 m) long for sewing.

1.

Whipped Cream (make 3)

With F, ch 28.

Row 1: (2 dc) in 4th ch, dc in next 22 ch, dc2tog, turn—25 dc.

Work whipped cream in BLO through end.

Row 2: Ch 3, dc2tog, dc in next 22 dc, (2 dc) in next dc, turn—25 dc.

Row 3: Ch 3, (2 dc) in next dc, dc in next 22 dc, dc2tog, turn—25 dc.

Rows 4–18: Rep rows 2 and 3 seven times more, then rep row 2 once more.

Row 19: Ch 1, bring the edge of row 18 and the foundation ch together to form a tube and sl st them together. Fasten off, leaving a tail 1 yd (1 m) long.

Turn the tube inside out so that the seam from the sl sts is on the inside of the tube.

Close one end of the tube, weaving tapestry needle threaded with yarn tail in and out of the edge of open end, skipping every other row. Pull on the yarn to close the opening. A spiral pattern will form. Tie off to secure, but don't fasten off. (**Photo 1**)

Insert needle into the center of the opening just closed and pass the needle through to the open side of the tube. Close this end in the same manner. Fasten off and weave in ends.

Cherry (make 3)

With G, ch 3, join with sl st to form ring. Place marker for beg of rnd.

Rnd 1: Work 6 sc in ring. Do *not* join.

Rnd 2: (2 sc) in each sc around—12 sc.

Rnd 3: [(2 sc) in next sc, sc in next sc] 6 times—18 sc.

Rnd 4: Sc in each sc around.

Rnd 5: [(2 sc) in next sc, sc in next 2 sc] 6 times—24 sc.

Rnds 6–7: Sc in each sc around.

Rnd 8: [invdec, sc in next 2 sc] 6 times—18 sc.

Rnd 9: Sc in each sc around.

Stuff with polyester stuffing.

Rnd 10: [invdec, sc] 6 times—12 sc.

Cont to stuff cherry firmly.

Rnd 11: [invdec] 6 times, join with sl st in next st.

Fasten off, leaving a tail 12" (30.5 cm) long. Thread tail through remaining 6 sts and pull to close. Weave in ends.

Cherry Stem

With G, ch 17, leaving a long tail.

Row 1: Sl st in 2nd ch from hook, sl st in next 15 ch, being sure to work in both loops of each ch. Fasten off leaving a tail 24" (61 cm) long.

Thread tail through top and out bottom of the cherry, being sure to pull the tail completely through, so that it dangles beneath the cherry. Thread the beginning tail as for the end tail, letting the needle exit 1 st away from center of last rnd. Pull firmly on both tails to anchor stem. Stem should not pass all the way though the cherry, and most of it should stick out of the top. Tie a knot, weave in the shorter tail, and keep the longer one for sewing.

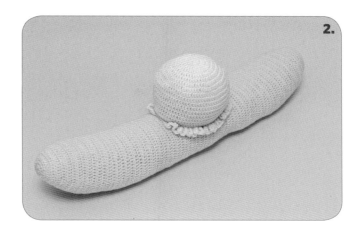

2.

Assembly

Sew center ice cream scoop to center top of banana, using the long tail of center ice cream scoop and a running st. Make sure that the 2 places without ruffles are oriented toward the sides of the scoop, where the side ice cream scoops will be sewn. Take care not to sew down the ruffles. (**Photo 2**)

Place or pin 1 side ice cream scoop next to the center ice cream scoop, making sure that the place without ruffles is facing the center ice cream scoop. Sew side ice cream scoop to the banana.

Sew 2nd side ice cream scoop to the banana in the same way.

Sew a cherry to the top and center of each whipped cream.

Sew a whipped cream to the top and center of each hot fudge sauce.

Sew a hot fudge sauce to the top and center of each ice cream scoop, leaving some of the bottoms of the drips free to curl.

Glue mini pompoms on whipped cream for sprinkles.

cheeseburger tissue box cozy

The first time I crocheted a cheeseburger tissue box cozy was for the 2012 Plush You! art show which is founded and annually curated by my friend Kristen. Ever since then, people have been writing to me for the pattern, and now I'm excited to serve it up with a juicy patty, frilly lettuce, tomato slices, onion strings, cheesey goodness, and even cute little sesame seeds on the top bun. Your tissues will become a talking point, and you will be the first person you know with a cube-shaped burger to impress all the gourmet-burger fanatics! If anybody happens to shed happy tears over the savory amazingness of this cozy, you'll already have something handy to wipe them away.

INGREDIENTS

(4) worsted weight

Lion Brand Vanna's Choice, 100% Premium Acrylic, 3.5 oz (100 g)/170 yds (156 m) per skein: 1 skein 860-130 Honey (A)

Red Heart Soft, 100% Acrylic, 5 oz (141 g)/256 yds (234 m) per skein: 1 skein #E728-9344 Chocolate (C)

Small amounts of worsted weight acrylic yarn: 10 yds (10 m) Beige (B), 5 yds (5 m) Green (D), 9 yds (9 m) Yellow (E), 6 yds (6 m) Red (F), 6 yds (6 m) White (G)

Small amount light tan wool felt OR small amount of B for sesame seeds

TOOLS

H/8 (5.00 mm) crochet hook
cube-shaped tissue box
tapestry needle
fabric glue (if using felt for sesame seeds)
stitch marker

DIRECTIONS

Gauge
17 sts x 21 rows in sc = 4" (10 cm).
Take time to check gauge.

Finished Size
4.75" (12 cm) wide x 4.75" (12 cm) long x 5.25" (13.5 cm) high

Special Stitches Used
DOUBLE TREBLE CROCHET (DTR)
Yo 3 times, insert hook in st, yo and draw up a loop, [yo and draw through 2 loops on hook] 4 times.

Note: The top of the cozy is worked first in rows. Then, work is continued in rnds for the sides.

Bun and Burger
With A, ch 19.

Row 1: Sc in 2nd ch from hook, sc in each ch across, turn—18 sc.

Rows 2–10: Ch 1, sc in each sc across, turn.

Row 11: Ch 1, sc in next 4 sc, ch 10 (for opening), sk 10 sts, and sc in next 4 sc, turn—18 sts.

Rows 12–20: Ch 1, sc in each sc across, turn. Do *not* turn at end of row 20. Do *not* fasten off.

BEGIN SIDES

Rnd 1: Ch 1, sc 19 evenly along side of square, sc 18 across foundation ch, sc 19 evenly along 2nd side of square, sc in next 18 sc, join with sl st to 1st sc, turn—74 sc. Place marker for beg of rnd.

Rnds 2–8: Ch 1, sc in each sc around, join with sl st to 1st sc, turn.
Fasten off A. Join B.

Rnd 9: Ch 1, sc in each sc around, join with sl st to 1st sc, turn.
Fasten off B. Join C.

Rnds 10–18: Ch 1, sc in each sc around, join with sl st to 1st sc, turn.
Fasten off C. Join B.

Rnd 19: Rep rnd 9.
Fasten off B. Join A

Rnds 20–27: Rep rnds 10–17.
Fasten off and weave in ends.

Lettuce
With RS facing and cozy facing right side up, join D to beg of rnd in the first B rnd up from the bottom of the cozy. (**Photo 1**)

Rnd 1: *[Ch 4, sk 1 st, sl st in B st] 3 times, [ch 6, sk 1 st, sl st in B st] once. rep from * around, ch 4 sk 1 st, sl st in 1st st to join. Fasten off and weave in ends.

Cheese (make 3)
With E, ch 2.

Row 1: (3 sc) in 2nd ch from hook, turn—3 sc.

Row 2: Ch 2, (hdc, sc) in first sc, sc in next, (sc, hdc) in next sc, turn—5 sts.

Row 3: Ch 2, (hdc, sc) in next st, sc in next 3 sts, (sc, hdc) in next st, turn—7 sts.

Row 4: Ch 3, sc in next 6 sts, (sc, dc) in next st—8 sts. Do *not* turn.

Border row: Ch 1, work 6 sl st along the side of the piece, (sl st, ch 1, sl st) in point, work 6 sl st along opposite side. Fasten off, leaving a tail 24" (61 cm) long for sewing, and weave in short end.

2.

Assembly

Place cozy on tissue box. Arrange cheese slices as desired along the upper B row. Whipstitch top of cheese slice to B row, then using straight sts, sew down cheese edges.

TOMATOES

Join F in st to the left of a cheese slice.

Row 1: Ch 3, sk 3 sts on cozy, work 1 dtr in the 4th st, (ch 3, dtr into same st as previous dtr) twice, ch 3, sk 3 sts on cozy, sl st in the 4th st. Fasten off and weave in ends. Rep for 2 more tomatoes.

ONIONS

Cut a 2 yd (2 m) strand of G and join to cozy 2 spaces to the right of the left side of tomato (between the center and left of tomato).

Row 1: Ch 18, sk 8 sts, sl st to the 9th st on cozy, sl st in next st on cozy, ch 18, sl st in st to the left of joining. Rep for 2 more onions, being sure that they reach the cheese slices.

(Photo 2)

SESAME SEEDS

Cut sesame seeds out of wool felt and attach to top of cozy with fabric glue as desired. OR embroider sesame seeds to top of cozy with B.

licorice allsorts afghan

I had never made an afghan before I designed this one! If this is also your first afghan, you're in for a treat. I've always loved the bright, bold colors of licorice allsorts candies. Their simple shapes and stripes make for two square motifs that we can use to create a fabulous candy blanky. Start small (12 squares for a small afghan) or go big (as many as you want). Drape it over your favorite armchair or cover the whole couch. We'll use six colors to represent our candies, but ultimately the color combos are entirely up to you!

INGREDIENTS

 worsted weight

Red Heart Super Saver Economy, 100% Acrylic, 7 oz (198 g)/364 yds (333 m) per skein: 3 skeins E300-312 Black, 1 skein each #E300-706 Perfect Pink, #E300-254 Pumpkin, #E300-324 Bright Yellow, #E300-672 Spring Green, #E300-311 White

TOOLS

I/9 (5.5 mm) crochet hook
tapestry needle
stitch marker

DIRECTIONS

Gauge

One square = Approx 9" (23 cm) x 9" (23 cm)
Take time to check gauge.

Finished Size

Sample is 6 squares x 5 squares: approx 54 in. (137 cm) x
45 in. (114 cm)

Special Stitches Used

DOUBLE TREBLE CROCHET (DTR)
Yo 3 times, insert hook in next stitch. yo and draw up a loop,
[yo and draw through 2 loops on hook] 4 times.

HALF DOUBLE TREBLE CROCHET (HDTR)
Yo 3 times, insert hook in next stitch, yo and draw up a loop,
[yo and draw through 2 loops on hook] twice, yo and draw
through remaining 3 loops on hook.

Circle in a Square

*Note: In the sample, Black is used for all final rnds for a consistent
border. Make squares to match the candies, in the following
combinations: Black center with pink outer; black center with
yellow outer, white center with black outer.*

COLOR SEQUENCE
Center = A
Outer = B
Accent = C
Border = Black
(**Photo 1**)

CIRCLE IN A SQUARE (MAKE 15)
With A, ch 3, join with sl st to form ring. Place marker for
beg of rnd.

Rnd 1: Ch 2, 12 dc in ring, join with sl st in 1st dc—12 dc.

Rnd 2: Ch 2, (2 dc) in same st as joining, dc in next 11 dc, fasten
off A, join B as you sl st to 1st dc.

Rnd 3: Ch 2, (2 dc) in same st as joining, dc in next dc, [(2 dc) in
next dc, dc in next dc] 11 times, join with sl st in 1st dc
—36 dc.

Rnd 4: Ch 2, (2 dc) in same st as joining, 2 dc in next dc,
[(2 dc) in next, dc in next 2 dc] 11 times, join with sl st in 1st
dc—48 dc.

Rnd 5: Ch 2, (2 dc) in same st as joining, dc in next 3 dc, [(2 dc)
in next, dc in next 3 dc] 11 times, join with sl st in 1st dc
—60 dc.

Rnd 6: Ch 2, (2 dc) in same st as joining, dc in next 4 dc, [(2 dc)
in next, dc in net 4 dc] 11 times, fasten off B, join C with sl st
in 1st dc—72 dc.

Rnd 7: Ch 1, sc in same st as joining, [sc in next 2 dc, hdc in next
2 dc, dc in next 2 dc, htr in next dc, tr in next dc, (hdtr, 3 dtr,
hdtr) in next dc, tr in next dc, htr in next dc, dc in next 2 dc,
hdc in next 2 dc, sc in next 3 dc] 3 times, sc in next 2 dc, hdc
in next 2 dc, dc in next 2 dc, htr in next dc, tr in next dc, (hdtr,
3 dtr, hdtr) in next dc, tr in next dc, htr in next dc, dc in next
2 dc, hdc in next 2 dc, sc in next 2 dc, join with sl st to 1st
sc—88 sts.

Rnd 8: Ch 1, sc in same st as joining, [sc in next 5 sts, hdc in
next 3 sts, dc in next 2 sts, (5 dc) in next st, dc in next 2 sts,
hdc in next 3 sts, sc in next 6 sts] 3 times, sc in next 5 sts,
hdc in next 3 sts, dc in next 2 sts, (5 dc) in next st, dc in next
2 sts, had in next 3 sts, sc in next 5 sts, fasten off C, join Black
with sl st in 1st sc—104 sts.

Rnd 9: Ch 2, dc in same st as joining, [dc in next 12 sts, (5 dc) in
next st, dc in next 13 sts] 3 times, dc in next 13 sts, (5 dc) in
next st, dc in next 12 sts, join with sl st in 1st—120 sts.

Fasten off and weave in ends.

Striped Square

Make squares using colors as desired, using black for the 2nd
and 4th stripes, and the border.

COLOR SEQUENCE
Stripe 1 = D
Stripe 2 = Black
Stripe 3 = E
Stripe 4 = Black
Stripe 5 = F
Border = Black
(**Photo 2**)

STRIPED SQUARE (MAKE 15)
With D, ch 28, loosely.

Row 1: Hdc in 3rd ch from hook, hdc in next 25 ch, turn—26 hdc.

Rows 2–4: Ch 2, hdc in each hdc across, turn. Fasten off D.
Join Black

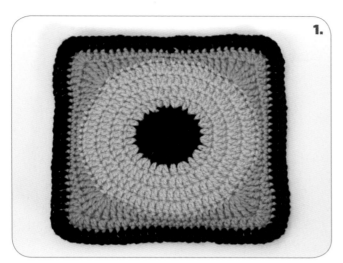

1.

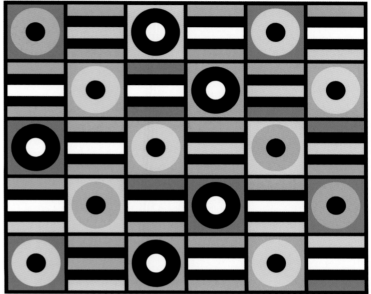

2.

Assembly

Smooth squares with hands, or block. Arrange squares as desired in 6 rows of 5 squares each. Whipstitch together using tails from striped squares.

Border

With Black, dc evenly around entire edge of blanket, working 5 dc in each corner and being sure the border lies flat. If you find that your border dips inward where your squares join, you can work a taller stitch, like a htr or tr, into the divot to even out the edge.

Rows 5–8: Rep row 2. Fasten off Black. Join E.
Rows 9–12: Rep row 2. Fasten off E. Join Black.
Rows 13–16: Rep row 2. Fasten off Black. Join F.
Rows 17–20: Rep row 2. Fasten off F. Join Black.
Border rnd: Ch 2, [dc in next 25 dc, (5 dc) in next st] 4 times around—120 dc.
Fasten off, leaving a tail 24" (61 cm) long for sewing, and weave in ends.

giant donut floor pouf

It's no secret: I LOVE DONUTS. My classic favorite is a glazed twist, but I'm also crazy for donuts covered in breakfast cereal, donuts stuffed with custard, and donuts decorated like cute animals! A few years ago, I crocheted some colorful animal donuts and wore them like little hats, but I've always wanted to design a giant donut floor pouf for my living room. I know my fellow donut lovers will also delight in having this super-sized treat to lounge on. Your guests will be fighting over who gets the sweetest seat!

INGREDIENTS

(**6**) super bulky weight

Lion Brand Hometown USA, 100% Acrylic, 5 oz (142 g)/81 yds (74 m) per skein: 5 skeins #135-102 Honolulu Pink (A), 7 skeins #135-159 Madison Mustard (B), 1 skein #135-099 Los Angeles Tan (C)

Red Heart Super Saver Economy, 100% Acrylic, 7 oz (198 g)/364 yds (333 m) per skein: small amounts each in assorted colors for sprinkles

TOOLS

M/13 (9.00 mm) crochet hook
H/8 (5.00 mm) crochet hook
tapestry needle
stitch marker
four 32 oz (900 g) bags polyester stuffing

DIRECTIONS

Gauge

9 sts x 11 rows in sc with larger hook = 4" (10 cm).
Take time to check gauge.

Finished Size

26" (6 cm) diameter x 15" (38 cm) high

Notes:

1) If you've never crocheted a donut shape before, it is recommended to do a trial run through the pattern with regular worsted weight yarn and an H hook.

2) Donut is worked from the inner hole to the outer edge, and then back to the hole.

3) RS shows on outside of donut.

Donut

With A and larger hook, ch 54. Join with sl st to 1st ch to form ring, being careful not to twist ch. Place marker for beg of rnd.

Rnd 1: Ch 1, sc in each ch around—54 sc. Do *not* join, rather work in a continuous spiral.

Rnds 2–15: Sc in each sc around.

Rnd 16: [(2 sc) in next sc, sc in next 5 sc] 9 times—63 sc.

Rnd 17: [(2 sc) in next sc, sc in next 6 sc] 9 times—72 sc.

Rnd 18: [(2 sc) in next sc, sc in next 7 sc] 9 times—81 sc.

Rnd 19: [(2 sc) in next sc, sc in next 8 sc] 9 times—90 sc.

Rnd 20: [(2 sc) in next sc, sc in next 9 sc] 9 times—99 sc.

Rnd 21: [(2 sc) in next sc, sc in next 10 sc] 9 times—108 sc.

Rnd 22: [(2 sc) in next sc, sc in next 11 sc] 9 times—117 sc.

Rnd 23: [(2 sc) in next sc, sc in next 12 sc] 9 times—126 sc.

Rnd 24: [(2 sc) in next sc, sc in next 13 sc] 9 times—135 sc.

Rnd 25: [(2 sc) in next sc, sc in next 14 sc] 9 times—144 sc.

Rnd 26: [(2 sc) in next sc, sc in next 15 sc] 9 times—153 sc.

Rnd 27: [(2 sc) in next sc, sc in next 16 sc] 9 times—162 sc.

Rnds 28–33: Sc in each sc around.

Rnd 34: Sc in each sc around, join with sl st in next st.

Rnd 35: Working in FLO, sl st in each st around, keeping sts loose and even, join with sl st in 1st sl st.

Fasten off A. Join B.

Rnd 36: Working in BLO, sc in each st in rnd 34. Do *not* join. (**Photo 1**).

Rnds 37–41: Sc in each sc around.

Rnd 42: Sc in each sc around, join with sl st in next st. Fasten off B. Join C.

Rnds 43–44: Sc in each sc around.

Rnd 45: Sc in each sc around, join with sl st in next st. Fasten off C. Join B.

Rnds 46–59: Sc in each sc around.

Rnd 60: [invdec, sc in next 16 sc] 9 times—153 sc.

Rnd 61: [invdec, sc in next 15 sc] 9 times—144 sc.

Rnd 62: [invdec, sc in next 14 sc] 9 times—135 sc.

Rnd 63: [invdec, sc in next 13 sc] 9 times—126 sc.

Rnd 64: [invdec, sc in next 12 sc] 9 times—117 sc.

Rnd 65: [invdec, sc in next 11 sc] 9 times—108 sc.

Rnd 66: [invdec, sc in next 10 sc] 9 times—99 sc.

Rnd 67: [invdec, sc in next 9 sc] 9 times—90 sc.

Rnd 68: [invdec, sc in next 8 sc] 9 times—81 sc.

Rnd 69: [invdec, sc in next 7 sc] 9 times—72 sc.

Rnd 70: [invdec, sc in next 6 sc] 9 times—63 sc.

Rnd 71: [invdec, sc in next 5 sc] 9 times—54 sc.

Rnds 72–90: Sc in each sc around, join with sl st in next st.

Fasten off, leaving a tail 1 yd (1 m) long for sewing (**Photo 2**). Weave in short end of foundation ch.

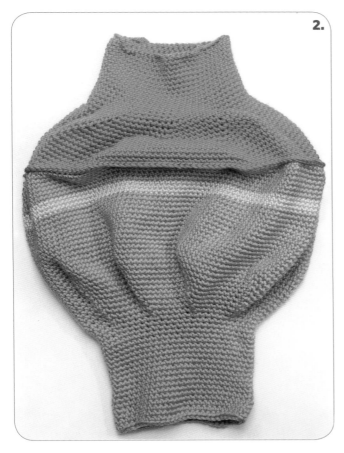

2.

3.

Sprinkles (make 22)

With smaller hook and desired color, ch 3, join with sl st to 1st ch to form ring. Place marker for beg of rnd.

Rnd 1: Ch 1, work 8 sc in ring—8 sc. Do *not* join, rather work in a continuous spiral.

Rnd 2: Sc in each sc around.

Rep rnd 2, stuffing lightly as you go, until piece is 3.5" (9 cm) long, join with sl st in next st. Fasten off, leaving a tail 24" (61 cm) long. Thread tail through 8 sts and pull to close. Weave in the short end.

Assembly

Whipstitch the last rnd of donut to foundation ch, using 1 yd (1 m) of A at a time and stuffing donut as you go. (**Photo 3**).

Sew 10 sts at a time and be sure that stuffing is full and smooth before sewing further.

Sew sprinkles to donut as desired.

bath & beauty

Don't forget to make time to pamper yourself and re-charge.
Let's turn your bathroom into a sanctuary of sweetness and celebration!
Gummy bears, ice cream cones, birthday cakes, bubble gum,
with a cherry on top, all functional and fun. . . **even the cherries!**

gummy bear towel basket

Have you ever wished that you could find glitter-yarn in any color and any weight? I have exciting news! You can make your own by combining regular yarn with shimmery metallic thread, which is perfect for candy-themed projects that need a bit of twinkle. This glittery gummy bear towel basket will hold your rolled, clean towels with sweetness and sparkle. You can also use the basket in other rooms to hold socks, toys, snacks, or even more yarn! It's even big enough to hold your favorite small quilts and throw blankets. I picked green because that's my favorite gummy flavor, but the materials I'm using come in a rainbow of candy colors to match your linens *and* your candy cravings!

INGREDIENTS

(4) worsted weight

Red Heart Super Saver Classic, 100% Acrylic 100%, 3.5 oz (100 g)/190 yds (174 m) per skein: 2 skeins #E300-672 Spring Green (A)

Sulky Holoshimmer Metallic Thread, Polyester, 250 yds (228.5 m) per spool: 4 spools #6032 Lime Green (B)

TOOLS

M/13 (9.00 mm) crochet hook
tapestry needle
stitch marker
straight pins

DIRECTIONS

Gauge

9 sts x 11 rows in sc with 2 strands each of A and B
held together = 4" (10 cm).

Take time to check gauge.

Note that adding B does not affect the gauge and can
be eliminated if desired.

Finished Size

34" (86.5 cm) circumference x 17.5" (44.5 cm) long, from
top of ear to floor

Notes:

*1. Project is worked with 2 strands of A and 2 strands of B held
together throughout (**Photo 1**).*

2. Basket is worked from the bottom up.

1.

Body

Ch 3, join with sl st in 1st ch to form ring.

Rnd 1: Ch 1, work 1 sc, 9 hdc in ring—10 sts. Do *not* join rnds,
rather work in a continuous spiral. Place marker for beg
of rnd.

Rnd 2: (2 hdc) in each st around—20 hdc.

Rnd 3: [(2 hdc) in next hdc, hdc in next hdc] 10 times—30 hdc.

Rnd 4: [(2 hdc) in next hdc, hdc in next 2 hdc] 10 times
—40 hdc.

Rnd 5: [(2 hdc) in next hdc, hdc in next 3 hdc] 10 times
—50 hdc.

Rnd 6: [(2 hdc) in next hdc, hdc in next 4 hdc] 10 times
—60 hdc.

Rnd 7: [(2 hdc) in next hdc, hdc in next 5 hdc] 10 times—70 hdc.

Rnd 8: [(2 hdc) in next hdc, hdc in next 6 hdc] 9 times, (2 hdc)
in next hdc, hdc in next 4 hdc, sc in next 2 hdc, join with sl st
in next st—80 st.

BEGIN SIDES

Rnd 9: Ch 1 and sc in BLO in same st as joining, hdc in BLO of
next 79 hdc. Do not join.

Rnds 10–24: Hdc in each hdc around—80 hdc.

Rnd 25: [hdc2tog, 6 hdc] 10 times—70 hdc.

Rnd 26: [hdc2tog, 5 hdc] 10 times—60 hdc.

Rnd 27: [(2 hdc) in FLO of next hdc, hdc in FLO in next 5 hdc]
10 times—70 hdc.

Rnd 28: [(2 hdc) in both loops of next hdc, hdc in both loops of
next 6 hdc] 10 times—80 hdc.

Rnds 29–36: Hdc in each hdc around.

Rnds 37–38: Rep rnds 25–26—60 hdc.

Rnd 39: Sc in next 2 hdc, sc2tog, sc in next 5 hdc, sc2tog, sc in
next 4 hdc, sc2tog, sl st in next st, sk 2 sts, (8 tr) in next hdc,
sk 2 sts, sl st in next hdc, sc in next 2 hdc, sc2tog, sc in next
3 hdc, sc2tog, sc in next 2 hdc, sl st in next hdc, sk 2 sts,
(8 tr) in next hdc, sk 2 sts, sl st in next hdc, sc2tog, sc in next
4 hdcc, sc2tog, sc in next 5 hdc, sc2tog, sc in next 2 hdc, join
with sl st to next st.—57 sts. Fasten off and weave in ends.

Ovals for Eyes and Nose (make 3)

Ch 5.

Rnd 1: Hdc in 3rd and 4th ch, (5 hdc) in last ch, working in
opposite side of foundation ch, hdc in next ch, (4 hdc) in the
last ch, join with sl st in 1st hdc—12 hdc.

Fasten off, leaving a tail 24" (60 cm) long for sewing, and weave
in short end.

Snout

Ch 6.

Rnd 1: Hdc in 3rd ch from hook, hdc in next 2 ch, (5 hdc) in last ch, working in opposite side of foundation ch, hdc, in next 2 ch, (4 hdc) in last ch, join with sl st in 1st hdc—14 sts. Place marker for beg of rnd.

Rnd 2: Ch 2, (2 hdc) in same st as joining, hdc in next 2 hdc, (2 hdc) in next 5 hdc, hdc in next 2 hdc, (2 hdc) in next 4 hdc, join with sl st in 1st hdc—24 hdc.

Rnd 3: Ch 2, (2 hdc) in same st as joining, hdc in next 3 hdc, [(2 hdc) in next hdc, hdc in next hdc] 5 times, hdc in next 2 hdc, [(2 hdc) in next hdc, hdc in next hdc] 4 times join with sl st in 1st hdc—34 hdc.

Fasten off, leaving a tail 1 yd (1 m) for sewing, and weave in short end.

Assembly

Sew nose to snout, using 1 strand of A.

Pin eyes and snout to top of body and sew down, using 1 strand of A. (**Photo 2**)

birthday cake toilet paper cozy

Grandma Wendleton—my best friend's grandma who taught me to crochet when I was ten years old—made classic toilet paper cozies that looked like dolls in dresses, complete with plastic doll torsos on top and crocheted skirts hiding the toilet paper roll inside. Let's give Grandma's TP cozies a fun update by turning them into playful birthday cakes! I've included both a jumbo cozy and a smaller cozy to accommodate your various TP needs. Between birthdays, housewarmings, Mother's Day, and the holiday season, you'll have plenty of opportunities to cover everyone's powder room in sprinkles and cheer! Add some vanilla or strawberry-scented room spray for a multi-sensory experience!

INGREDIENTS

(4) worsted weight

Red Heart Classic, 100% Acrylic, 3.5 oz (100 g)/190 yds (174 m) per skein: 1 skein #E267-681 Mist Green (A)

Red Heart Super Saver Economy, 100% Acrylic, 7 oz (198 g)/364 yds (333 m) per skein: 37 yds (34 m) #E300-37 Petal Pink (B)

Worsted weight acrylic yarn for each candle: 6 yds (6 m) White (C), 3 yds (3 m) Teal (D), and 2 yds (2 m) Yellow (E)

5-mm mini pompoms

TOOLS

G/6 (4.00 mm) crochet hook
H/8 (5.00 mm) crochet hook
tapestry needle
stitch markers
straight pins
fabric glue (for sprinkles)

DIRECTIONS

Gauge

15 sts x 18 rows in sc with A and larger hook = 4" (10 cm). Take time to check gauge.

Finished Size

Jumbo roll: 6" (15 cm) diameter x 4.25" (11 cm) high, excluding candles

Regular roll: 5.25" (13.5 cm) diameter x 4.25" (11 cm) high, excluding candles

Special Stitches Used

TALL POPCORN

[Yo] twice, insert hook into next st, yo and draw up a loop, [yo and draw through 2 loops on hook] twice, *yo twice, insert hook into same st, yo and draw up a loop, [yo and draw through 2 loops on hook] twice; rep from * twice more, yo and draw through all 5 loops on hool.

Note: Instructions for cake portion of small cozy are given first, cake portion of jumbo cozy follow. Borders, candles and assembly are the same for both sizes.

Small Cozy

With larger hook and A, ch 3, join with sl st to form ring. Place marker for beg of rnd.

Rnd 1: Ch 2, 10 hdc in ring, join with sl st in 1st st—10 hdc.

Rnd 2: Ch 2, (2 hdc) in each hdc around, join with sl st in 1st st—20 hdc.

Rnd 3: Ch 2, [(2 hdc) in next hdc, hdc in next hdc] 10 times, join with sl st in 1st st—30 hdc.

Rnd 4: Ch 2, [(2 hdc), in next hdc, hdc in next 2 hdc] 10 times, join with sl st in 1st st—40 hdc.

Rnd 5: Ch 2, [(2 hdc) in next hdc, hdc in next, 3 hdc] 10 times, join with sl st in 1st st—50 hdc.

Rnd 6: Ch 1, [(2 sc) in next hdc, sc in next 9 hdc] 5 times, join with sl st in 1st st to join—55 sc.

Rnd 7: Ch 1, sc in next sc, hdc in each rem sc. Do *not* join.

Rnds 8–18: Hdc in each st around.

Rnd 19: Sc in next 55 sts, join with sl st in next st.

Fasten off and weave in ends. Begin shell border top.

Jumbo Cozy

Work as for small cozy through rnd 5.

Rnd 6: Ch 2, [(2 hdc) in next hdc, hdc in next, 4 hdc] 10 times, join with sl st in 1st st—60 hdc.

Rnd 7: Ch 2, [(2 hdc) in next hdc, hdc in next, 5 hdc] 10 times, join with sl st in 1st st—70 hdc.

Rnd 8: Ch 1, sc in next hdc, hdc in rem hdc. Do *not* join.

Rnds 9–19: Hdc in each st around. Do *not* join.

Rnd 20: Sc in each st around, join with sl st in 1st st. Fasten off and weave in ends.

Shell Border Top

With larger hook and B, ch 2.

Row 1: Sc in 2nd ch from hook, turn—1 sc.

Row 2: Ch 3, tall popcorn in next st, turn.

Row 3: Ch 1, sc in next st.

Rep rows 2 and 3 until border fits around the top edge of cozy being sure to have an even number of tall popcorns. Fasten off, leaving 1 yd (1 m) for sewing.

Shell Border Bottom

Work as for shell border top until border fits around the bottom edge of cozy (approx 2 tall popcorns more).

Candle (make 3)

With larger hook and C, ch 3, leaving a tail 18" (45.5 cm) long at beg, join with sl st to form ring. Place marker for beg of rnd.

Rnd 1: Ch 1, work 6 sc in ring—6 sc. Do *not* join.

Rnd 2: Sc in each st around.

Rep rnd 2 until candle measures 3.75" (9.5 cm) long. Fasten off C.

FLAME

Change to smaller hook. Join E with sl st to beg of rnd.

Rnd 1: Ch 2, in BLO work as follows: [(2 hdc) in next st, hdc in next st] 3 times, join with sl st in 1st st—9 hdc.

Rnd 2: Ch 2, work in both loops as follows: [hdc2tog, hdc in next hdc] 3 times, join with sl st in 1st st—6 hdc.

Rnd 3: Ch 1, sc in each st around, join with sl st in 1st st.

Fasten off, leaving a tail 12" (30.5) long. Thread tail through the outside loops of the rem 6 sts and pull to close. Tie off and weave in all ends, excepting the beg tail.

SPIRAL

Join D to one end of candle and surface sl st or embroider a chain st, using photo as guide.

Assembly

Place cozy on toilet paper roll. Pin shell border top to top edge and sew down using a straight stitch in each sc, threading the yarn to the WS of the cozy behind each tall popcorn. Sew shell border bottom to bottom of cozy in the same way.

DROP STRINGS

With larger hook, join B with sl st in any sc in shell border top.

Rnd 1: *Ch 25, sk 1 sc, sl st in next sc; rep from * around. Fasten off and weave in ends.

Glue mini pompoms to top of cake as desired.

ATTACH CANDLES

Pin candles to top of cozy and sew with whipstitches. If your candles flop over too much, try sewing the second to last rnd (instead of the last rnd) of the candles to the cozy. This can provide more stability, but remember that crochet does produce a soft sculpture.

ice cream cone shower mitt

Are you tired of your store-bought shower puff unraveling and exploding into a useless pile of plastic? Let's crochet our own cute shower mitts and zap them with ice cream magic! Stick your hand into the bottom of the ice cream cone, pop your thumb out the thumb hole, and your fingers will become the scrubby ice cream scoops on top! If you share a bathroom with someone else, you can make a bunch of mitts in different colors and flavors to tell them apart. I chose a fun, fringed cotton yarn that mimics terry cloth for extra scrubbing action, but you can use whatever yarn you like as long as the gauge is the same. Beginners may want to practice with a regular, non-fuzzy yarn first, because the fringe can make the stitches difficult to see. However, the resulting fabric is pretty cool and worth the effort!

INGREDIENTS

(4) worsted weight

Red Heart Creme de la Creme, 100% Combed Cotton, 2.5 oz (70 g)/125 yds (114 m) per skein: 1 skein #0307 Tan (A), small amount #0905 Rally Red (D)

Mary Maxim Scrub It, 100% Cotton, 1.75 oz (50 g)/76 yds (69.5 m) per skein: 1 skein each #Y01107 Pink (B) and #Y01106 Lime (C)

TOOLS

H/8 (5.00 mm) crochet hook
tapestry needle
stitch marker

DIRECTIONS

Gauges

16 sts x 19 rows in sc with A = 4" (10 cm).
14 sts x 15 rows in sc with B = 4" (10 cm).
Take time to check gauge.

Finished Size

8" (12.5 cm) wrist diameter x 11" (28 cm) long,
excluding hanging loop

Special Stitches Used

HALF DOUBLE CROCHET 2 TOGETHER (HDC2TOG)
Yo, insert hook in next st, yo and draw up a loop, yo, insert hook
in next st, yo, draw through 1 loop on hook, yo, draw through all
5 loops on hook.

FRONT POST HALF DOUBLE CROCHET (FPHDC)
Yo, insert hook from front to back and to front again around the
vertical post of stitch on the previous row, yo and draw up a
loop, yo and draw through 3 loops on hook. Work the next st in
next st of previous row.

FRONT POST TRIPLE CROCHET (FPTR)
[Yo] twice, insert hook from front to back and to front again
around the vertical post of stitch on the previous row, yo and
draw up a loop, [yo, draw through 2 loops on hook] 3 times.
Work the next st in next st of previous row.

Cone

With A, ch 32 loosely, join with sl st to 1st ch, being careful not
to twist ch. Place marker for beg of rnd.

Rnd 1: Ch 1 sc in back bump of each ch, join with sl st in 1st sc,
turn—32 sc.

Rnds 2-3: Ch 1, sc in each sc around, join with sl st in 1st sc, turn.

Rnd 4 (RS): Ch 1, [sc in next 3 sc, FPtr in the next st 3 rnds
below (**Photo 1**)] 8 times, join with sl st in 1st sc, turn.

Rnds 5-7: Ch 1, sc in each st around, join with sl st in 1st sc, turn.

Rnd 8: Ch 1, [3 sc, FPtr into the FPtr from 4 rows below] 8 times,
join with sl st in 1st sc, turn.

Rnd 9: Ch 1, FPhdc in each st around, join with sl st in 1st sc, turn

Rnds 10-16: Rep rows 2-8.

Begin thumb opening

Rnd 17: Ch 1, FPhdc in next 27 sts, turn, leaving rem sts
unworked. Do *not* join.

Rnds 18-21: Ch 1, sc in next 27 sts, turn. Do *not* join.

Rnd 22: Ch 1, sc in next 27 sc, ch 5, join with sl st in 1st sc,
turn—32 sts

Rnd 23: Ch 1, sc in next 5 sts, FPhdc in next 27 sc, join with sl st
in 1st sc, turn.

Fasten off A. Join B.

Ice cream

Rnd 24 (RS): Ch 1, sc in each st around, join with sl st in
1st sc, turn.

Ruffle rnd: Work in BLO as follows: Ch 4, [(tr, ch 2, tr, ch 2) in
next st] 32 times, ch 2 once more, join sl st in 1st st,
turn—64 tr.

Rnd 25: Work in FLO of rnd 24, working behind ruffle as follows:
Ch 2, [(2 hdc) in next st, hdc in next 3 sts] 8 times, join with
sl st in 1st st, turn—40 hdc.

Rnds 26-28: Ch 2, hdc in each hdc around, join with sl st in 1st
st, turn—40 hdc.

Rnd 29: Ch 2, [hdc2tog, hdc in next hdc] 6 times, hdc2tog,
[hdc2tog, hdc in next hdc] 6 times, hdc2tog, join with sl st in
1st st, turn—26 hdc.

Fasten off B. Join C.

Rnd 30: Ch 1, [(2 sc) in next st, sc in next 3 sts, (2 sc) in next st,
sc in next 4 sts, (2 sc) in next st, sc in next 3 sts] twice, join
with sl st in 1st st, turn—32 sc.

Ruffle rnd: Work in FLO as follows: Ch 4, [(tr, ch 2, tr, ch 2) in
next st] 32 times, ch 2 once more, join with sl st in 1st st,
turn—64 tr.

Rnd 31: Work in BLO of rnd 30, working behind ruffle as follows: Ch 2, [(2 hdc) in next st, hdc in next 3 sts] 8 times, join with sl st in 1st st, turn—40 hdc.

Rnds 32-35: Ch 2, hdc in each hdc around, join with sl st in 1st st, turn—40 hdc.

Rnd 36: Rep rnd 29—26 hdc.

Rnd 37: Ch 2, [hdc2tog] 13 times, join with sl st in 1st st, turn—13 sts.

Rnd 38: Ch 1, [sc2tog] 6 times, sc in last st, join with sl st in 1st st, turn—7 sts.

Fasten off, leaving a tail 12" (24 cm) long. Thread tail through rem 7 sts and pull to close. Tie off and weave in ends.

Cherry

With D, ch 3 and join with sl st to 1st ch to form ring. Place marker for beg of rnd.

Rnd 1: Ch 1, 6 sc in ring—6 sc. Do *not* join.

Rnd 2: (2 sc) in each sc around—12 sc.

Rnd 3: [(2 sc) in next sc, sc in next 2 sc] 4 times—16 sc.

Rnds 4-5: Sc in each sc around.

Rnd 6: [invdec, sc in next 2 sc] 4 times—12 sc.

Fasten off, leaving a tail 18" (45.5 cm) long.

Make 2 small wads of stuffing by wrapping D yarn 20 times around 2 fingers. Stuff inside cherry. Trim or add more stuffing as necessary.

Rnd 7: With tail, [invdec] 6 times, join with sl st to next st.

Thread tail through rem 6 sts, pull to close. Tie off and weave in ends.

HANGING LOOP

With D, ch 35 leaving a tail 8" (12.5 cm) long at beg. Fasten off, leaving a tail 24" (61 cm) long for sewing. Thread both tails into the cherry top and out the bottom, enclosing the first chains on each end to form a loop. Weave in the short tail securely. Save the long tail for sewing the cherry to the mitt.

Assembly

Use the long tail to sew the cherry securely to the top of the mitt, sewing around entire bottom of the cherry.

little cherry zipper pulls

I have one of these cute cherry zipper pulls on my purse, and I love how the cherries add just a pop of color and sweetness to my bag. You can also put your cherry zipper pull on your makeup pouch, backpack, keychain, or jacket. If you're feeling bold, you can even turn the cherries into some cute dangly earrings (minus lobster clasp, plus earring findings)! This is a great project for stash-busting and takes hardly any time to complete!

INGREDIENTS

[4] worsted weight

Worsted weight yarn: 10 yds (10 m) Red (A) and 2 yds (2 m) Green (B)

TOOLS

H/8 (5.00 mm) crochet hook
G/6 (4.00 mm) crochet hooks
tapestry needle
small lobster clasp clip (9 mm x 23 mm available on Etsy.com)
stitch marker

1.

DIRECTIONS

Gauge

16 sts x 19 rows in sc with larger hook = 4" (10 cm).
Take time to check gauge.

Finished Size

Approx 1" (2.5 cm) diameter
3" (7.5 cm) long, including stem

Cherry (make 2)

With larger hook and A, leaving a tail 1 yd (1 m) long for stuffing, ch 3, join with sl st to form ring. Place marker for beg of rnd.

Rnd 1: Work 6 sc in ring—6 sc.

Rnd 2: (2 sc) in each ch around—12 sc.

Rnds 3-4: Sc in each sc around.

Rnd 5: [invdec 4 times], wrap beginning tail tightly around finger and stuff inside cherry, trim if necessary, [invdec] twice more, join with sl st in 1st sc—6 sc.

Fasten off, leaving a tail 12" (30.5 cm) long. Thread tail through outside loops of rem 6 sts and pull to close. Weave in end.

Cherry Stem

With smaller hook and B, leaving an 8" (12.5 cm) tail, ch 40, tightly. Ch measures approx 6.25" (16 cm) long. Fasten off, leaving an 8" (12.5 cm) tail.

Assembly

Thread tapestry needle with yarn tail from cherry stem and thread through center of rnd 1 through the center of rnd 5, drawing enough of the cherry stem through so that the last ch is hidden in the bottom of the cherry, and tie to the bottom of the cherry with a double knot. Weave in end.

Thread tapestry needle with 2nd tail from cherry stem, and draw stem through base of lobster clasp so that a little more than half the chain passes through the clasp. Thread the tapestry needle through the ch just below base of lobster clasp and draw the chain through. (**Photo 1**). To further secure, pass the stem through another 2 chs.

Attach stem to the 2nd cherry in the same manner.

bubble gum bath mat

Let's make a sweet treat for your feet! I'm prescribing you a double-bubble relaxation experience: first, a bubble bath, and then, this bubble gum bath mat! I was inspired by old-school, individually wrapped gum inside bright and colorful waxed papers with the twisted ends. You'll be using the loop stitch a lot in this pattern to create a cool vintage texture. The fun lettering in the middle will definitely give your bathroom some pop!

INGREDIENTS

 worsted weight

Lion Brand Kitchen Cotton, 100% Cotton, 2 oz (57 g)/99 yds (90 m) per skein: 5 skeins #831-157 Citrus (B), 2 skeins each #831-113 Hot Pepper (A), and #831-148 Tropic Breeze (C), 1 skein #831-098 Vanilla (D)

TOOLS

I/9 (5.5 mm) crochet hook
tapestry needle
stitch marker
straight pins

DIRECTIONS

Gauge

14 sts x 15 rows in sc = 4" (10 cm).
Take time to check gauge.

Finished Size

35" (89 cm) wide x 21" (53.5 cm) long

Special Stitches Used

LOOP STITCH (LP ST)

Note: lp st is a variation of sc that forms a loop at the back of the fabric.

Hold yarn over index finger 1.5" (4 cm) behind work, insert hook in st, hook both strands of yarn of loop just made and draw through st (3 loops on hook), (**Photo 1**), remove finger from loop, yo and draw through all 3 loops on hook to complete the st.

1.

Gum Ball

With A, ch 3, join with sl st to form ring.

Rnd 1 (WS): Ch 1, work 6 sc in ring—6 sc. Do *not* join. Place marker for beg of rnd.

Rnd 2: (2 sc) in each sc around—12 sc.

Rnd 3: [(2 sc) in next sc, sc in next sc] 6 times—18 sc.

Rnd 4: [Sc in next sc, (2 sc) in next sc, sc in next sc] 6 times —24 sc.

Rnd 5: [Sc in next 3 sc, (2 sc) in next sc] 6 times—30 sc

Rnd 6: [Sc in next 2 sc, (2 sc) in next sc, sc in next 2 sc] 6 times—36 sc.

Rnd 7: [(2 sc) in next sc, sc in next 5 sc] 6 times—42 sc.

Rnd 8: [Sc in next sc, sc in next 3 sc, (2 sc) in next sc, sc in next 3 sc] 6 times—48 sc.

Rnd 9: [(2 sc) in next sc, sc in next 7 sc] 6 times—54 sc.

Rnd 10: [4 sc in next sc, (2 sc) in next sc, sc in next 4 sc] 6 times—60 sc.

BEGIN LP ST

Rnd 11: [(2 lp st) in next sc, lp st in next 9 sc] 6 times—66 sts.

Rnd 12: [lp st in next 5 sts, (2 lp st) in next st, lp st in next 5 sts] 6 times—72 sts.

Rnd 13: [(2 lp st) in next st, lp st in next 11 sts] 6 times—78 sts.

Rnd 14: [lp st in next 6 sts, (2 lp st) in next st, lp st in next 6 sts] 6 times—84 sts.

Rnd 15: [(2 lp st) in next st, lp st in next 13 sts] 6 times. —90 sc

Rnd 16: [lp st in next 7 sts, (2 lp st) in next st, lp st in next 7 sts] 6 times—96 sts.

Rnd 17: [(2 lp st) in next st, lp st in next 15 sts] 6 times—102 sts.

Rnd 18: [lp st in next 8 sts, (2 lp st) in next st, lp st in next 8 sts] 6 times—108 sts.

Rnd 19: [(2 lp st) in next st, lp st in next 17 sts] 6 times—114 sts

Rnd 20: [lp st in next 9 sts, (2 lp st) in next st, lp st in next 9 sts] 6 times—120 sts.

Fasten off A. Join B.

BEGIN SC

Rnd 21: [(2 sc) in next sc, sc in next 19 sc] 6 times—126 sc.

Rnd 22: [Sc in next 10 sc, (2 sc) in next, sc in next 10 sc] 6 times—132 sc.

Rnd 23: [(2 sc) in next, sc in next 21 sc] 6 times—138 sc.

Rnd 24: [Sc in next 11 sc, (2 sc) in next sc, sc in next 11 sc] 6 times—144 sc.

Rnd 25: [(2 sc) in next sc, sc in next 23 sc] 6 times—150 sc.

Rnd 26: [Sc in next 12 sc, (2 sc) in next sc, sc in next 12 sc] 6 times—156 sc.

Rnd 27: [(2 sc) in next sc, sc in next 25 sc] 6 times—162 sc.

Rnd 28: [Sc in next 13 sc, (2 sc) in next sc, sc in next 13 sc] 6 times—168 sc.

Rnd 29: [(2 sc) in next sc, sc in next 27 sc] 6 times—174 sc.

Rnd 30: [Sc in next 14 sc, (2 sc) in next sc, sc in next 14 sc] 6 times—180 sc.

BEGIN LP ST

Rnd 31: [(2 lp st) in next st, lp st in next 29 sts] 6 times —186 sts.

Rnd 32: [lp st in next 15 sts, (2 lp st) in next st, lp st in next 15 sts] 6 times—192 sts.

Rnd 33: [(2 lp st) in next st, lp st in next 31 sts] 6 times—198 sts.

Rnd 34: [lp st in next 16 sts, (2 lp st) in next st, lp st in next 16 sts] 6 times—204 sts.

Rnd 35: [(2 lp st) in next st, lp st in next 33 sts] 6 times —210 sts.

Rnd 36: [lp st in next 17 sts, (2 lp st) in next st, lp st in next 17 sts] 6 times—216 sts.

Rnd 37: [(2 lp st) in next st, lp st in next 35 sts] 6 times —222 sts.

Rnd 38: [lp st in next 18 sts, (2 lp st) in next st, lp st in next 18 sts] 6 times—228 sts.

Rnd 39: [(2 lp st) in next st, lp st in next 37 sts] 6 times —234 sts.

Rnd 40: [lp st in next 19 sts, (2 lp st) in next st, lp st in next 19 st] 6 times, join with sl st in next st—240 sts.

Fasten off B. Join C.

First Gum Wrapper

Row 1: With C, ch 1, sc in same st as joining, sc in next 19 sts, turn—20 sc.

Row 2: Ch 2, (2 dc) in each st across, turn—40 sc.

Row 3: Ch 2, (2 dc) in each st across, turn—80 sc.

Rows 4-10: Ch 2, dc in each dc across, turn. Fasten off.

Second Gum Wrapper

With loopy side of gum ball facing you, join C in 101st st from last st of 1st gum wrapper. Work as for 1st wrapper. Fasten off and weave in ends.

P (make 2)

Note: Be sure to work sl sts loosely, as they will be worked in the next row.

With D, ch 21.

Row 1: Sc in 2nd ch from hook, sc in next 19 ch, turn—20 sc.

Rows 2-4: Ch 1, sc in each sc across, turn.

Row 5: Ch 1, sc in next 4 sc, turn leaving rem sts unworked —4 sc.

Rows 6-8: Ch 1, sc in each sc across, turn.

Row 9: Ch 2, dc in next sc, hdc in next sc, sc in next sc, sl st in next sc, turn.

Row 10: Ch 1, sl st in next st, sc in next st, hdc in next st, dc in next st.

Rows 11-19: Rep rows 9-10 four times more, then rep row 9 once.

Rows 20-22: Ch 1, sc in each st across, turn.

Fasten off, leaving a tail 1 yd (1 m) long for sewing, and weave in short end.

Use long yarn tail to whipstitch row 22 to row 4 to complete the "P".

O

Note: Be sure to work sl sts loosely, as they will be worked in the next row.

With D, ch 5 for bottom of "O".

Row 1: Sc in 2nd ch from hook, sc in next 3 ch—4 sc.

Row 2: Ch 1, sc in each sc across, turn.

Row 3: Ch 1, sl st in next sc, sc in next sc, hdc in next sc, dc in next sc, turn—4 sts.

Row 4: Ch 2, dc in next st, hdc in next st, sc in next st, sl st in next st.

Rows 5-7: Rep rows 3-4 once more, then rep row 3.

Rows 8-16: Ch 1, sc in each sc across, turn.

Rows 17-21: Rep rows 3-7.

Rows 22-24: Ch 1, sc in each sc across, turn.

Rows 25-29: Rep rows 3-7.

Rows 30-38: Ch 1, sc in each sc across, turn.

Rows 39-43: Rep rows 3-7.

Fasten off, leaving a tail 1 yd (1 m) long for sewing, and weave in the short end.

Use long yarn tail to whipstitch 1st and last rows together to complete the "O".

Assembly

Arrange letters on mat using photo as guide. Pin in place.

Beginning with the letter O, sew the word "POP" to the center of the gumball.

home office

Whether you're working or in school, at home or at the office, a little bit of cheer on your desk can definitely perk up your day. Sign that important document with a corn dog pen or organize your special memos in a squishy bread loaf. Take a coffee break and bring your tablet with you, protected in a cozy that looks like a retro TV dinner. Work doesn't have to be boring.

You'll see when everyone smiles at your playful and delectable new gear!

TV dinner tablet cozy

I'm crazy about the retro look of TV dinners from the 50s and 60s. As a kid growing up in the 80s, we ate a Swanson meal here and there, but it was such a rare occasion that the experience always seemed novel and fun to me. So I thought it would be cool to bring that vintage, tin-tray aesthetic to a piece of today's technology by making a cozy for my iPad Mini that looks like a Salisbury steak dinner, complete with peas and buttery, whipped potatoes!

INGREDIENTS

4 worsted weight

Lion Brand Vanna's Choice, 100% Premium Acrylic,
3.5 oz (100 g)/170 yds (156 m) per skein: 1 skein #860-405
Silver Heather (A), 20 yds (19 m) #860-124 Toffee (B),
22 yds (20 m) #840-098 Lamb (D), 3 yds (3 m) #840-157
Duckie (E)

Red Heart Soft, 100% Acrylic, 5 oz (141 g)/265 yds (234 m)
per skein: 12 yds (11 m) #E728-9344 Chocolate (C)

Cascade Yarns 220, 100% Peruvian Highland Wool, 3.5 oz
(100 g)/220 yds (200 m) per skein: 30 yds (28 m)
8903 Primavera (F)

TOOLS

H/8 (5.00 mm) crochet hook

G/6 (4.00 mm) crochet hook

.75" (19 mm) button

tapestry needle

small amount of polyester stuffing

straight pins

stitch marker

sewing needle and thread

hot glue gun and clear hot glue sticks for fabric, and tinfoil to
protect cozy from glue (optional)

DIRECTIONS

Gauge

16 sts x 19 rows in sc with larger hook = 4" (10 cm).
Take time to check gauge.

Finished Size

6" (15 cm) wide x 8.5" (21.5 cm) long

Cozy

Note: After working 4 rnds, place on tablet to check fit and adjust if necessary.

With A and larger hook and leaving a tail 24" (61 cm) long for sewing, ch 48 or enough to fit around the width of your tablet, join with sl st to form ring, being careful not to twist ch. Place marker for beg of rnd.

Rnd 1: Sc in each ch—48. Do *not* join rnd, rather, work in a continuous spiral.

Rnd 2: Sc in each sc around.

Rep rnd 2 until cozy measures 8.5" (21.5 cm) long, or 1 rnd longer than your tablet.

Button loop rnd: Sc in next 11 sc, sl st into next st, ch 25 tightly and sl st into next st sc in next rem sc, sl st in 1st st to join. Beg of rnd is side of cozy and button loop is at center.

Fasten off and weave in short tail.

Whipstitch bottom of cozy closed using the beginning tail.

Tray Edge A

With A and larger hook, ch 8, join with sl st in first ch, being careful not to twist ch.

Rnd 1: Sc in each ch—8 sc. Do *not* join rnds. Place marker for beg of rnd.

Rnd 2: Sc in each sc around.

Rep rnd 2 until tube measures 27" (68.5 cm) long or fits all the way around the top edge of the cozy, join with sl st to next st.

Fasten off, leaving a tail 18" (45.5 cm) long. Use tail to sew 1st and last rnds of tube together. Weave in ends.

Tray Edge B

Work as for tray edge A until tube measures 1.75" (4.5 cm) long, join with sl st in next st.

Fasten off, leaving a tail 18" (45.5 cm) long for sewing.

Tray Edge C (make 2)

Note: Be sure that both tray edge C pieces are the same length to form the upside-down Y shape with tray edge B. The exact length or number of rnds is not important. Work as for tray edge A until tube measures 4.5" (11.5 cm) long, join with sl st to next st.

Fasten off, leaving a tail 18" (45.5 cm) long for sewing.

Steak

With B and larger hook, ch 3 and join with sl st to form ring. Place marker for beg of rnd.

Rnd 1: Ch 1, work 8 sc in ring—8 sc. Join with sl st in first ch, being careful not to twist ch.

Rnd 2: (2 sc) in each sc around—16 sc.

Rnd 3: [(2 sc) in next sc, sc in next sc] 8 times—24 sc.

(continued)

Rnds 4–16: Sc in each sc around.

Rnd 17: [invdec, sc in next sc] 8 times—16 sc.

Stuff lightly.

Rnd 18: [invdec] 8 times, join with sl st in next st—8 sc.

Fasten off, leaving a tail 12" (30.5 cm) long.

Thread tail through rem 8 sts and pull to close. Tie off and weave in ends.

GRILL MARKS

Using photo as guide and C, embroider long diagonal sts on top of steak.

Sauce

With C and larger hook, ch 16.

Rnd 1: Hdc in 3rd ch from hook, hdc in next 12 ch, (5 hdc) in last ch, working in opposite side of foundation chain, hdc in next 12 hdc, (4 hdc) in last ch—34 hdc. Place marker for beg of rnd.

Rnd 2: (2 hdc) in next, hdc in next 12 hdc, (2 hdc) in next 5 hdc, hdc in next 12 hdc, (2 hdc) in next 4 hdc—44 hdc.

Rnd 3: (2 hdc) in next hdc, hdc in next 13 hdc, [(2 hdc) in next hdc, hdc in next hdc] 4 times, (2 hdc) in next hdc, hdc in next 13 hdc, [(2 hdc) in next hdc, hdc in next hdc] 4 times —54 hdc.

Rnd 4 (forms angled edge): [(2 sc) in next sc, sc in next 2 sc] twice, hdc in next hdc, dc in next hdc, htr in next hdc, tr in next 4 hdc, htr in next hdc, dc in next hdc, hdc in next hdc, sc in next hdc, sl st in next st.

Fasten off, leaving a tail 1 yd (1 m) long for sewing, and weave in other end.

Whipped Potatoes (make 2)

With D and larger hook, ch 7.

Row 1: Sc in 2nd ch from hook, sc in next 5 ch, turn—6 sc.

Row 2: Ch 1, sc in each sc across, turn.

Row 3: Ch 1, (2 sc) in next sc, sc in next 5 sc, turn—7 sc.

Row 4: Ch 1, sc in each sc across, turn.

Row 5: Ch 1, (2 sc) in next sc, sc in next 6 sc—8 sc.

Row 6: Ch 1, sc in each sc across, turn.

Row 7: Ch 1, (2 sc) in next sc, sc in next 7 sc, turn—9 sc.

Row 8: Ch 1, sc in each sc across, turn.

Row 9: Ch 1, (2 sc) in next sc, sc in next 8 sc—10 sc.

Row 10: Ch 1, sc in each sc across, turn.

Row 11: Ch 1, (2 sc) in next sc, sc in next 9 sc—11 sc.

Row 12: Ch 1, sc in each sc across, turn.

Row 13: Ch 1, (2 sc) in next sc, sc in next 10 sc—12 sc.

Rows 14–15: Ch 1, sc in each sc across, turn.

Fasten off and weave in ends. Leave a tail 1 yd (1 m) long on 2nd piece for sewing.

Butter Pat

With E and larger hook, ch 5.

Row 1: Sc in 2nd ch from hook, sc in next 3 ch, turn—4 sc.

Rows 2–4: Ch 1, sc in each ch across, turn.

Border rnd: Ch 1, sl st evenly around entire square as follows: 4 sl st across top, 3 sl st along 1st side, 4 sl st across bottom, 3 sl st along 2nd side, join with sl st to 1st st.

Fasten off, leaving a tail 24" (61 cm) long sewing, and weave in rem end.

Peas

Note: WS shows on outside of peas.

With F and smaller hook, ch 3.

Rnd 1: Working through both loops of ch, work (8 hdc) in last ch, join with sl st—8 hdc.

Rnd 2 (WS): Ch 2, [hdc2tog] 4 times, join with sl st in 1st hdc, sk next st, and sl st in following st. 1st pea is complete.

Rnd 3: Ch 5, working through both loops of ch, work (8 hdc) in 3rd ch from hook, join with sl st in first hdc, letting previous pea fall to back—8 hdc. (**Photo 1**).

Rnd 4 (WS): Ch 2, [hdc2tog] 4 times. Complete as for 1st pea.

Rep rnds 3–4 twenty-two times more (for 24 peas) or until your string of peas is 22" (56 cm) long. Drape the peas into the tray as you go to determine how many to make. Peas should cover same area as the whipped potatoes, with some for a 2nd layer to add dimension.

Fasten off, leaving a tail 1 yd (1 m) for sewing.

Assembly

Notes: The side with the button loop is the top of cozy. Hot glue may be used for assembly instead of sewing, taking care to place a piece of tinfoil between the layers of the cozy, so that the glue doesn't seep through.

TRAY EDGES

Pin and then sew tray edge A around the perimeter of the top of the cozy, being careful to not to sew through both layers of cozy. (**Photo 2**).

Position, pin, and sew tray edge B first to the inside edge of tray edge A and then to the cozy itself.

Position both tray edge C pieces. Sew the ends to tray edge B where all the tray pieces meet in the middle. Then, pin and sew both tray edge C pieces to the inner edges of tray edge A, and then to the cozy.

STEAK AND SAUCE

Place sauce inside largest section of the tray. The slightly pointed edge should fit snugly in the top and center of tray section. Sew sauce to cozy. Position and pin the steak to the center of the sauce, sew in place.

WHIPPED POTATOES

Whipstitch both whipped potato pieces together to form a small pillow, stuffing lightly before sewing closed. Join D to any top corner of the whipped potatoes, and surface sc to create a zig-zag design. Sew butter pat to top. Sew whipped potatoes to inside edges of tray.

PEAS

Zig-zag 1 layer of peas into tray. Sew to cozy through the sts between the peas. Arrange remaining peas to form a 2nd layer and sew to the 1st layer. Weave in ends.

BUTTON

Place tablet inside cozy. Pull the button loop over the opening to the back of cozy and mark for the center of button with pin. Sew the button in place. (**Photo 3**)

taco pencil case

One of my earliest and proudest DIY moments was back in junior high when I hand-sewed my own pencil case out of felt and then puffy-painted a bunch of Yellow No. 2 pencils all over it. These days, I collect cute pencil cases to use as crochet tool kits, so I really wanted to design a fun pencil case for this book. I polled friends and fans on social media to choose between a zippered pouch that looked like a watermelon or a taco, and tacos won by a landslide! This project is perfect not only for small school supplies or crochet tools, but also makeup or special little keepsakes. The crocheted pencil case is felted (or fulled) to close up the holes in the stitches and create more of a solid, strong fabric. This can sometimes be an intimidating process for a first-timer, but felting is an exciting transformation and I think you'll have a lot of fun experimenting once you get going!

INGREDIENTS

(4) worsted weight

Cascade Yarns 220, 100% Peruvian Highland Wool, 3.5 oz (100 g)/220 yds (200 m) per skein: 1 skein each #8686 Brown (A), #7828 Neon Yellow (B), #8903 Primavera (C), #8414 Bright Red (D); 12 yds (11 m) #7825 Orange Sherbet (E)

TOOLS

H/8 (5.00 mm) crochet hook
I/9 (5.50 mm) crochet hook

12" (30.5 cm) yellow zipper to match taco shell
tapestry needle
straight pins
sewing needle and thread to match taco shell, lettuce, tomato, and cheese
zippered pillow case (or regular pillow case and rubber band), old towels, and a dryer (for the dryer-method of felting)
plastic shopping bags (for blocking, if needed)

DIRECTIONS

Gauges

14 sts x 17 rows in sc with larger hook = 4" (10 cm).
19 sts x 23 rows in sc with smaller hook = 4" (10 cm).
Take time to check gauge.

Finished Size

5.5" (14 cm) wide x 11.5" (29 cm) long x 2.5" (6.5 cm) deep, after felting

Notes: Pieces that will be felted should be worked loosely. The felted parts of the taco are worked with a larger hook.

Meat

With A and larger hook, ch 2.
Row 1: Sc in last ch, turn—1 sc.
Row 2: Ch 1, sc in next sc, turn.
Row 3: Ch 1, (2 sc) in next sc, turn—2 sc.
Row 4: Ch 1, sc in each sc across, turn.
Row 5: Ch 1, (2 sc) in next sc, sc in next sc, turn—3 sc.
Row 6: Ch 1, sc in each sc across, turn.
Row 7: Ch 1, sc in next 2 sc, (2 sc) in next sc—4 sc.
Row 8: Ch 1, sc in each sc across, turn.
Row 9: Ch 1, (2 sc) in next sc, sc in next 3 sc—5 sc.
Row 10: Ch 1, sc in each sc across, turn.
Row 11: Ch 1, sc in next 4 sc, (2 sc) in next sc—6 sc.
Row 12: Ch 1, sc in each sc across, turn.
Row 13: Ch 1, (2 sc) in next sc, sc in next 5 sc—7 sc.
Row 14: Ch 1, sc in each sc across, turn.
Row 15: Ch 1, tsc in next 6 sc, (2 sc) in next sc, turn—8 sc
Row 16: Ch 1, sc in each sc across, turn.

Row 17: Ch 1, (2 sc) in next sc, sc in next 7 sc, turn—9 sc.
Row 18: Ch 1, sc in each sc across, turn.
Row 19: Ch 1, sc in next 8 sc, (2 sc) in next sc—10 sc.
Row 20: Ch 1, sc in each sc across, turn.
Row 21: Ch 1, (2 sc) in next sc, sc in next 9 sc—11 sc.
Row 22: Ch 1, sc in each sc across, turn.
Row 23: Ch 1, sc in next 10 sc, (2 sc) in next sc—12 sc.
Row 24–50: Ch 1, sc in each sc across, turn.
Row 51: Ch 1, sc2tog, sc in next 10 sc—11 sc.
Row 52: Ch 1, sc in each sc across, turn.
Row 53: Ch 1, sc in next 9 sc, sc2tog—10 sc.
Row 54: Ch 1, sc in each sc across, turn.
Row 55: Ch 1, sc2tog, sc in next 8 sc—9 sc.
Row 56: Ch 1, sc in each sc across, turn.
Row 57: Ch 1, sc in next 7 sc, sc2tog—8 sc.
Row 58: Ch 1, sc in each sc across, turn.
Row 59: Ch 1, sc2tog, sc in next 6 sc—7 sc.
Row 60: Ch 1, sc in each sc across, turn.
Row 61: Ch 1, sc in next 5 sc, sc2tog—6 sc.
Row 62: Ch 1, sc in each sc across, turn.
Row 63: Ch 1, sc2tog, sc in next 4 sc—5 sc.
Row 64: Ch 1, sc in each sc across, turn.
Row 65: Ch 1, sc in next 3 sc, sc2tog—4 sc.
Row 66: Ch 1, sc in each sc across, turn.
Row 67: Ch 1, sc2tog, sc in next 2 sc—3 sc.
Row 68: Ch 1, sc in each sc across, turn.
Row 69: Ch 1, sc in next sc, sc2tog—2 sc.
Row 70: Ch 1, sc in each sc across, turn.
Row 71: Ch 1, sc2tog.
Row 72: Ch 1, sc in next sc.
Fasten off and weave in ends.

(continued)

First Taco Shell

Note: Meat is attached to each taco shell when working rnd 25.
With B and larger hook, ch 3, join with sl st in 1st ch to form ring.

Row 1: Ch 1, work 3 sc in ring, turn—3 sc.

Row 2: Ch 1, (2 sc) in next 3 sc, turn—6 sc.

Row 3: Ch 1, [(2 sc) in next sc, sc in next sc] 3 times, turn—9 sc.

Row 4: Ch 1, [(2 sc) in next sc, sc in next 2 sc] 3 times, turn—12 sc.

Row 5: Ch 1, [(2 sc) in next sc, sc in next 3 sc] 3 times, turn—15 sc.

Row 6: Ch 1, [(2 sc) in next sc, sc in next 4 sc] 3 times, turn—18 sc.

Row 7: Ch 1, [(2 sc) in next sc, sc in next 5 sc] 3 times, turn—21 sc.

Row 8: Ch 1, [(2 sc) in next sc, sc in next 6 sc] 3 times, turn—24 sc.

Row 9: Ch 1, [(2 sc) in next sc, sc in next 7 sc] 3 times, turn—27 sc.

Row 10: Ch 1, [(2 sc) in next sc, sc in next 8 sc] 3 times, turn—30 sc.

Work 14 rows more in this manner, increasing 3 sc in each row, varying the placement of the increases to create a smooth half-circle—72 sc at the end of row 24.

JOIN MEAT TO TACO SHELL

Place meat on top of taco shell with the long edge of the meat lined up with the curved edge of the taco shell, insert hook in the end of meat row 1 and then into the 1st st of taco shell. Work row 25 in both the next st of meat and the next st of taco shell to join the pieces together (**Photo 1**).

Row 25: Ch 1, sc in next 16 sc, (2 sc) in next sc, sc in next 19 sc, (2 sc) in next sc, sc in next 18 sc, (2 sc) in next sc, sc in next 16 sc, turn—75 sc.

Rnd 26: Ch 1, [(2 sc) in next sc, sc in next 24 sc] 3 times, turn—78 sc.

Rnd 27: Ch 1, sc in next 18 sc, [(2 sc) in next, sc in next 19 sc] 3 times, turn—81 sc.

Rnd 28: Ch 1, [sc in next 26 sc, (2 sc) in next sc] 3 times—84 sc.

Fasten off, leaving a tail 12" (30.5 cm) long for sewing and weave in other end.

Taco shell measures approx 14" (35.5 cm). It will shrink when felted.

Second Taco Shell

Make same as first taco shell, joining 2nd side of meat when working row 25.

Lettuce (make 2)

With C and smaller hook, ch 56.

Row 1: Sc in 2nd ch from hook, sc in next 54 ch, turn—55 sc.

Row 2: Ch 2, (dc, ch 2, dc, ch 2) in each st across, after last ch 2, join with sl st to the same st.

Fasten off and weave ends.

Tomato (make 9)

With D and smaller hook, leaving a 12" (30.5 cm) tail, ch 5.

Row 1: Sc in 2nd ch from hook, sc in next 3 ch, turn—4 sc.

Rows 2–9: Ch 1, sc in each sc across, turn.

Fasten off, leaving a tail 12" (30.5 cm) long for sewing.

Fold piece to from square. Whipstitch the sides of the square together and weave in ends.

Cheese Shreds (make 9)

With E, ch 13.

Row 1: Working through both loops of ch, sl st in 2nd ch from hook and in each ch to end. Fasten off and weave in ends.

Assembly

Using 12" (30.5 cm) tails, whipstitch the top edges of the taco shells together for 1" (2.5 cm) on each side. Weave in ends. (**Photo 2**)

FELT TACO SHELL AND MEAT

Soak piece in cold water, making sure it is thoroughly wet and place it in zippered pillowcase to protect dryer. Place pillowcase and some wet towels in dryer. Set dryer to the highest temperature. The longer the taco is left in the dryer, the more it will shrink and the smoother it will be. If the taco dries out before you are satisfied with the level of felting, wet it again and give it more time in the dryer. The sample was kept tumbling for a total of 100 minutes, re-soaking the project at the start of every 25-minute cycle.

If necessary block the taco as follows: Soak taco again and carefully squeeze out excess water by hand. Place taco between two dry towels and roll. Re-shape the project with your hands and stuff plastic bags inside so that the meat panel dries flat and the pouch has dimension. Let dry completely; this may take more than one day.

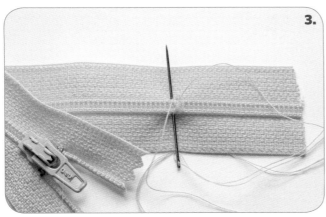

LETTUCE
When taco is completely dry, pin the foundation ch of each lettuce to the meat, along the inner edges of the taco shell. Begin pinning at the center of work your way along each side. Sew to meat using needle and thread to match the lettuce.

TOMATOES
Arrange tomatoes and pin in place. With needle and thread to match tomato, sew 1 edge or corner of each tomato down allowing remaining portion of tomato to be unattached.

CHEESE
Arrange cheese shreds and pin in place. With needle and thread to match cheese shreds, sew each cheese shred to meat through the center of cheese shred, allowing ends to stick out.

ZIPPER
Lay the zipper across the flat edge of the taco and to what length of zipper you need. If the zipper needs to be shortened, use needle and thread to create a new stop as follows: Sew several stitches around the zipper teeth and trim the zipper approx 1" (2.5 cm) from new stop (**Photo 3**). Pin the cloth edges of zipper to taco opening and sew the zipper in. (**Photo 4**)

carnival pen cozies

What's the best part about summertime, carnivals, and theme parks? The junk food! These corn dog and cotton candy pen cozies will make doing homework and office work a billion times more awesome. The cozies are removable, so once the pen runs out of ink, you can just put in a new pen. There's one to satisfy your sweet tooth and one to satisfy that savory craving, so everyone wins!

INGREDIENTS

(4) worsted weight

Corn Dog and Bitten Corn Dog

Lion Brand Vanna's Choice, 100% Premium Acrylic,
    3.5 oz (100 g)/170 yds (156 m) per skein: 7 yds (7 m)
    #860-123 Beige (A), 24 yds (22 m) #860-135 Rust (B)
3 yds (3 m) of worsted weight yarn for mustard or ketchup

Bitten Corn Dog only

3 yds (3 m) of worsted weight yarn in Pink (C)
4 yds (3.5 m) of worsted weight yarn in Mustard (D)

Cotton Candy

Lion Brand Vanna's Choice, 100% Premium Acrylic,
    3.5 oz (100 g)/170 yds (156 m) per skein: 7 yds (7 m)
    #860-100 White (E),
Cascade Yarns 220, 100% Peruvian Highland Wool, 3.5 oz
    (100 g)/220 yds (200 m) per skein: 25 yds (23 m) #9477
    Tutu (pink F) OR #8908 Anis (blue F)

Note: Use 100% wool for the cotton candy. The results are not guaranteed if acrylic yarn is used.

TOOLS

H/8 (5.00 mm) crochet hook
I/9 (5.50 mm) crochet hook
pet slicker brush
polyester stuffing
ballpoint pen
stitch marker

DIRECTIONS

Gauges

16 sts x 19 rows in sc, with smaller hook and A = 4" (10 cm).
19 sts x 23 rows in sc, with smaller hook and F = 4" (10 cm).
Take time to check gauge.

Finished Size

Corn dog: 1.75" (4.5 cm) wide x 8" (10.5 cm) long
Cotton candy: 3" (7.5 cm) wide x 7" (18 cm) long

CORN DOG PEN COZY

Stick

With A and larger hook, ch 5, join with sl st to form ring.
    Place marker for beg of rnd.

Rnd 1: Work 5 sc in ring.

Rnd 2: Sc in each sc around.

Rep rnd 2 until piece measures 5" (12.5 cm) from beg.

It's ok for the WS to show on the outside.

Place tube on pen to check length.

Join with sl st and fasten off. Thread tail through last 5 sts to
    close. Weave in ends. Keeping opening at bottom loose.

Body

Note: RS shows on outside of body.

With smaller hook and B, ch 3, join with sl st to form ring.

Rnd 1: Work 6 sc in ring—6 sc. Do *not* join. Place marker for
    beg of rnd.

Rnd 2: (2 sc) in each sc around—12 sc.

Rnd 3: [(2 sc) in next sc, sc in next sc] 6 times—18 sc.

Rnd 4: [(2 sc) in next sc, sc in next 8 sc] twice—20 sc.

Rnds 5–22: Sc in each sc around.

Start stuffing the corn dog with polyester stuffing.

Rnd 23: [invdec, sc in next 2 sc] 5 times—15 sc.

Rnd 24: [invdec, sc in next sc] 5 times, join with sl st in next
    st—10 sc.

Fasten off leaving a tail 18" (45.5 cm) long for sewing.

Finish stuffing the body, being sure to stuff into the bottom
    corners of the corn dog, moving stuffing into the base with
    room for the stick. This keeps the body from wobbling around
    too much on the pen. (**Photo 1**)

Assembly

Place stick on pen and insert stick so that 1–1.5" (2.5–4 cm) is
inside the body. Some resistance against the stuffing is desirable
for stability. Sew body to stick.

Using photo as guide, add mustard or ketchup using
embroidered chain st or surface sl st, or crochet about 50 chains
and sew to corn dog as desired.

BITTEN CORN DOG PEN COZY

Stick

Work as for corn dog pen cozy.

Body

With smaller hook and C, ch 3, join with sl st to form ring.

Rnd 1: Work 6 sc in ring—6 sc.

Place a marker for beg of rnd and move marker up every rnd.
    RS shows on outside of corn dog.

Rnd 2: (2 sc) in each sc around, join with sl st in next st—12 sc.

Fasten off C. Join D.

Rnd 3: Working in BLO, ch 1, [(2 sc) in next 2 sc, sc in next sc]
    4 times, join with sl st—20 sc.

Rnd 4: Working in FLO, ch 1, sc in same st as joining, hdc in next
    st, dc in next 2 st, hdc in next st, sc in next 6 sts, hdc in next
    st, dc in next 2 sts, hdc in next st, sc in next 5 sts, join with
    sl st in 1st sc.

Fasten off D. Join B.

Rnd 5: Working in BLO, rep rnd 4. Note that rnd 4 aims upward, and rnd 5 aims downward, to create a ridge where the corn dog was "bitten."

Rnd 6: Working in both loops and in rem back loops of rnd 4 (**Photo 2**), rep rnd 5, This ensures that the "bite" in the corn dog stays propped up—20 sts. Do *not* join.

Weave in ends.

Rnd 7: Sc in each sc around. Do *not* join.

Rep rnd 7 fifteen times more.

Start stuffing the corn dog with polyester stuffing. Stuff lightly, just enough to keep the shape.

Complete as for whole corn dog, beg with rnd 23.

COTTON CANDY PEN COZY

Stick

With E, work as for corn dog pen cozy.

Body

Note: RS shows on outside of body.

With F and smaller hook, ch 3, join with sl st to form ring.

Rnd 1: Work 6 sc in ring—6 sc. Do *not* join.

Place marker for beg of rnd.

Rnd 2: (2 sc) in each sc around—12 sc.

Rnd 3: [(2 sc) in next sc, sc in next sc] 6 times—18 sc.

Rnd 4: [(2 sc) in next sc, sc in next 2 sc] 6 times—24 sc.

Rnds 5–6: Sc in each sc around.

Rnd 7: [(2 sc) in next sc, sc in next 3 sc] 6 times—30 sc.

Rnds 8–10: Sc in each sc around.

Rnd 11: [(2 sc) in next, sc in next 4 sc] 6 times—36 sc.

Rnds 12–16: Sc in each sc around.

Rnd 17: [invdec, sc in next 4 sc] 6 times—30 sc.

Rnd 18: [invdec, sc in next 3 sc] 6 times—24 sc.

Rnd 19: [invdec, sc in next 2 sc] 6 times—18 sc.

Brush the yarn with the slicker brush to create the fuzz on the cotton candy. Brush small areas at a time, brushing in all different directions with short and vigorous strokes. Brush as close to the base as possible before the body is sewn to the stick. (**Photo 3**) When brushing is complete, lightly stuff the body.

Rnd 20: [invdec, sc in next sc] 6 times—12 sc.

Brush out the bottom a little more and add a little more stuffing if desired.

Rnd 21: [invdec, sc in next 2 sc] 3 times, join with sl st in next st—9 sc.

Fasten off, leaving a tail 18" (45.5 cm) for sewing.

Assembly

Place stick on pen and insert stick so that 1–1.5" (2.5–4 cm) is inside the body. Some resistance against the stuffing is desirable for stability. Sew body to stick.

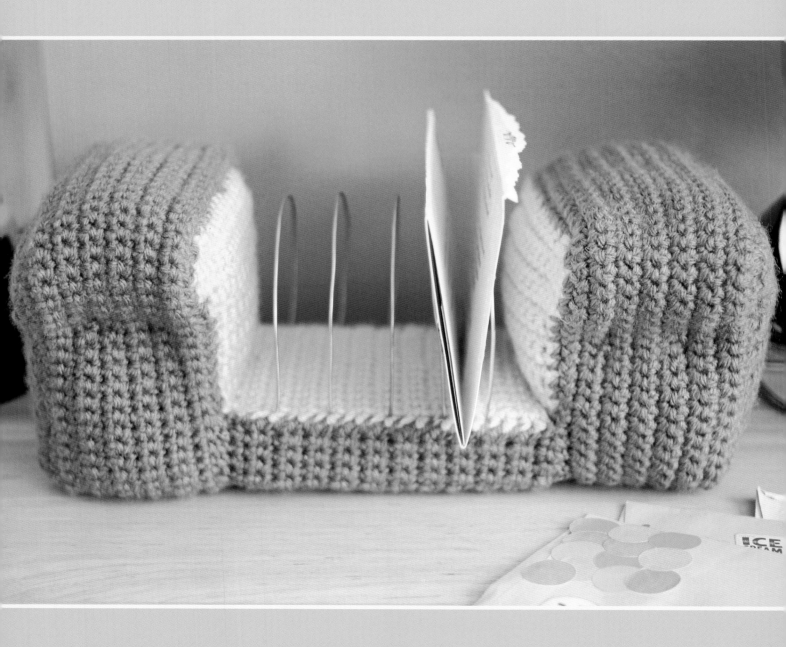

bread loaf letter organizer

My mom is a huge collector of my crocheted goodies. When Mother's Day rolls around, I always try to think of something new and fun to make for her. This Bread Loaf Letter-Organizer is actually the gift I designed for her for Mother's Day 2014. My parents get *a lot* of mail. I have no idea if this organizer can actually hold all of it, but even my dad said, "Hey, that's just what your mom needs!" If Dad approves, you know you have a winner! The mail at my childhood home lives in the kitchen, so I thought that a cute and squishy bread loaf would do nicely!

INGREDIENTS

 worsted weight

Lion Brand Vanna's Choice, 100% Premium Acrylic, 3.5 oz (100 g)/170 yds (156 m) per skein: 1 skein each #860-123 (A) Beige, #860-130 Honey (B)

TOOLS

H/8 (5.0 mm) crochet hook

tapestry needle

stitch marker

14 gauge jewelry wire (or a more heavy-duty wire of a similar gauge)

wire cutters

polyester stuffing

4" (10 cm) x 5" (12.5 cm) white florists foam 1" (2.5 cm) thick

serrated knife to cut foam

can or jar for shaping wire, craft glue (optional)

DIRECTIONS

Gauge

16 sts x 19 rows in sc = 4" (10 cm).
Take time to check gauge.

Finished Size

11" (28 cm) wide x 4.5" (11.5 cm) high x 6" (15 cm) deep

Bread Slice 1 (make 2)

With A, ch 15.

Row 1: Sc in 2nd ch from hook, sc in next 13 ch, turn—14 sc.

Rows 2-12: Ch 1, sc in next 14 sc, turn.

Row 13: Ch 1, (2 sc) in next 2 sc, sc in next 10 sc, (2 sc) in next 2 sc, turn—18 sc.

Row 14: Ch 1, (2 sc) in next sc, sc in next 16 sc, (2 sc) in next sc, turn—20 sc.

Row 15: Ch 1, sc in each sc across, turn.

Row 16: Ch 1, sc2tog, sc in next 16 sc, sc2tog, turn—18 sc.

Row 17: Ch 1, [sc2tog] twice, sc in next 10 sc, [sc2tog] twice —14 sc.

Fasten off A. Join B.

BORDER (**Photo 1**)

Border rnd: Ch 1, sc in next 13 sc, (2 sc) in next sc, (2 sc) in next 4 sts (around curve), sk next st, work 11 sc evenly along side of piece, (3 sc) in corner, sc in 12 sc across the bottom, (3 sc) in next st, sk the 1st st of the next side of piece, work 11 sc evenly along side, (2 sc) in next 4 sts (around curve), sc in the same st as 1st sc of rnd, join with sl st to 1st sc—72 sc.

Fasten off. Weave in ends.

Bread Slice 2 (make 2)

With B, work as for bread slice 1, working slice and border in B.

Bread Loaf End (make 2)

With RS of bread slice 2 facing you, join B into the bottom right corner of rnd 1.

Rnd 1: Ch 1, work 1 sc in each st, join with sl st to 1st sc to join, turn—72 sc. Place marker for beg of rnd.

Rnds 2-12: Rep rnd 1.

Fasten off, leaving a tail 38" (97 cm) long for sewing.

Whipstitch bread slice 1 to rnd 12 of bread slice 2, stuffing lightly before completing seam. Do not overstuff. Bread loaf end should look fluffy but doesn't need to be firm, otherwise the bottom won't lie flat.

SHAPING

Thread tapestry needle with 1 yd (1 m) of B. With the A (slice 1) side of piece facing you, insert tapestry needle into side at row 12 of bread slice and about 4 rnds into bread loaf end, and run needle through bread loaf end to opposite side. Staying at 4 rnds in, insert needle again in row 10 of the bread slice, then run the needle through to opposite side of. Gently pull and tie the 2 yarn ends together to create the bread loaf shape (**Photo 2**). Trim the yarn and weave in the ends. Turn piece over so that bread slice 2 is facing you, and repeat shaping.

Bread Base Top

With A, leaving a 24" (61 cm) tail, ch 15.

Row 1: Sc in 2nd ch from hook, sc in next 13 sc, turn—14 sc.

Rows 2-22: Ch 1, sc in each sc across, turn.

Fasten off leaving a tail 24" (61 cm) long for sewing.

Bread Base Bottom

With B, leaving a 1 yd" (1 m) tail, ch 27.

Row 1: Sc in 2nd ch from hook, sc in next 25 sc, turn—26 sc.

Rows 2-22: Ch 1, sc in each sc across, turn.

Fasten off leaving a tail 1 yd" (1 m) long for sewing.

Assembly

Place bread base top on foam block. With a pen, carefully trace bread base top and cut the foam block to size.

Place foam block between bread base top and bread base bottom. Use B tails on each side to whipstitch the edges of bread base top to bread base bottom. The short edges of the foam will remain exposed. Tie off but don't cut B yet. These yarn tails will be used later.

Arrange pieces as in **Photo 3** and whipstitch ends of bread base to each loaf end.

Cut 5 pieces of wire 10" (25.5 cm) long and bend into arches. Wrapping piece around a can or jar will help form an arch. Insert the arches into bread base, evenly spaced, to create partitions for letters. Dip ends in craft glue, if desired, to secure; but take care to arrange them first.

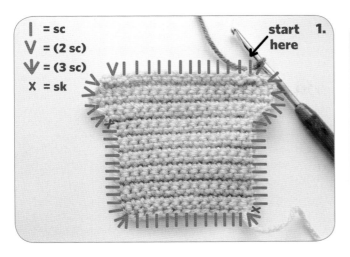

| = sc
V = (2 sc)
⩔ = (3 sc)
X = sk

start here 1.

2.

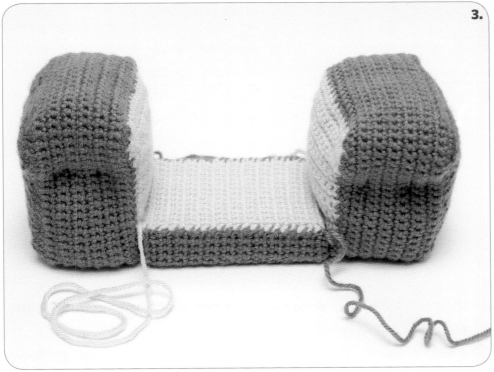

3.

red licorice wrist rest

When I polled my friends and fans on social media about an office item that they really wanted and needed, a keyboard wrist rest cozy was one of the most popular. Most of the office projects in this book have been on the savory side, so I wanted this last pattern to be sugary and sweet. Keyboard wrist rests come in a variety of sizes, and I picked one of the larger ones as my model so that the cozy might accommodate whatever size you happen to have in your office. You can also fill the cozy with polyester stuffing instead. Either way, I hope your sparkly new candy-coated wrist rest helps you comfortably complete your next big typing project, like maybe *your crochet book!*

INGREDIENTS

(4) worsted weight
Caron Simply Soft Party, 99% Acrylic, 1% Polyester, 3 oz (85 g)/164 yds (150 m) per skein: 2 skeins #0015 Red Sparkle

TOOLS

H/8 (5.00 mm) crochet hook
scissors
tapestry needle
stitch marker
18" (45.5 cm) x 3.25 (8 cm) wrist rest, or polyester stuffing
red dimensional fabric paint (optional)

DIRECTIONS

Gauge

17 sts x 20 rows in sc = 4" (10 cm).
Take time to check gauge.

Finished Size

19.75" (50 cm) wide x 3.5" (9 cm) long

Special Stitches Used

FRONT POST DOUBLE TREBLE CROCHET (FPDTR)
Yo 3 times, insert hook from front to back and to front again around the post of designated st, yo, draw up a loop, [yo, draw through 2 loops on hook] 4 times.

Red Licorice Wrist Rest

Ch 32, join with sl st to form ring, being careful not to twist ch. Place marker for beg of rnd.

Rnd 1: Ch 1, sc in each ch around, join with sl st in 1st st, turn—32 sc.

Rnds 2–3: Ch 1, sc in each ch around, join with sl st to 1st sc, turn.

BEGIN SWIRL PATTERN
(*Notes: The FPdtrs lean toward the right to create swirl effect. Remember not to work in st behind FPdtr just worked.*)

Rnd 4 (RS): Ch 1, sc in next 2 sc, FPdtr around 6th sc 3 rnds below (rnd 1), FPdtr around next st 3 rnds below (**Photo 1**), [sc in next 2 sts, FPdtr around 3rd sc 3 rnds below, FPdtr around next 3 rnds below] 7 times, join with sl st to 1st sc, turn—32 sts.

Rnds 5–7: Ch 1, sc in each sc around, join with sl st in 1st sc, turn.

Rnd 8: Ch 1, FPdtr around 2nd FPdtr 4 rnds below, sc in next 2 sts (**Photo 2**), *[FPdtr in next FPdtr 4 rnds below] twice, sc in next 2 sts; rep from * 6 times more, FPdtr in 1st FPdtr 4 rnds below, join with sl st in 1st st, turn.

Rnds 9–11: Ch 1, sc in each sc around, join with sl st in 1st sc, turn.

Rnd 12: Ch 1, FPdtr around 3rd FPdtr 4 rnds below (**Photo 3**), FPdtr around next FPdtr 4 rnds below, sc in next 2 sts, *[FPdtr around the next FPdtr from 4rd rnds below] twice, sc in next 2 sts; rep from * 6 times more, join with sl st, turn.

Rnds 13–15: Ch 1, sc in each sc around, join with sl st in 1st sc, turn.

Rnd 16: Ch 1, sc, FPdtr around 3rd FPdtr 4 rnds below, FPdtr around next FPdtr 4 rnds below, sc in next 2 sts *[FPdtr around next FPdtr 4 rnds below] twice, sc in next 2 sts; rep from * 5 times more, [FPdtr around next FPdtr 4 rnds below] twice, sc in next st, join with sl st to 1st st, turn.

Rnds 17–19: Ch 1, sc in each sc around, join with sl st in 1st sc, turn.

Rnd 20: Ch 1, 2 sc, FPdtr around 3rd FPdtr 4 rnds below, FPdtr around next FPdtr 4 rnds below, *sc in next 2 sts, [FPdtr around next FPdtr 4 rnds below] twice; rep from * 6 times more, join with sl st in 1st st, turn.

Rep rnds 5–20 to desired length of wrist rest, end with a rnd 20. Rep rnds 5–12 once more.

Last rnd: Ch 1, sc in each sc around, join with sl st in 1st sc. Do not fasten off, place a stitch marker in last loop to hold.

Assembly

Insert wrist rest, keeping working loop on the side of the wrist rest for ease in closing end. Once the wrist rest is completely inside the cozy, put your crochet hook back on the working loop and ch 2.

Close end by working 1 row of 16 hdc through both layers of fabric. (**Photo 4**).

Fasten off and weave in ends.

If using stuffing stuff cozy now.

Re-join yarn to open end, ch 2, and close as for other end.

Fasten off and weave in ends.

Apply dimensional fabric paint along some of the FPdtr stripes on bottom of cozy to keep cozy from slipping on desk. (**Photo 5**)

basic crochet instructions

CROCHET TOOL KIT

All crocheters have their favorite tools of the trade, and you'll slowly develop your own must-have equipment, but here are some basic items I would recommend to begin your crochet journey. I keep all my tools in a cute zipper pouch that looks like a banana!

→ **Hooks.** Crochet hooks come in different materials - like metal, plastic, or wood - and also different sizes. My Grandma Wendleton started me with a metal Susan Bates kit, and I've never looked back. These days, I buy the Susan Bates hooks with a bamboo handle, which I find more comfortable, but if you are just starting out, you can grab any basic crochet hook kit that will usually come with an F, G, H, I, J, and K hook. My favorite size to use is the H. Different hook brands might have slight differences in the hook shape that can affect how you crochet, so if one feels weird to you, you can try a different brand. The label on the yarn you're using will recommend a hook size, and that's a great place to start if you don't know what to buy and you just want to practice.

→ **Scissors.** Nothing fancy here. Just a small pair that will fit in your kit.

→ **Tapestry needle.** You'll be using a tapestry needle a lot for weaving the ends of your yarn into your work. You can find them in plastic or metal. I prefer metal ones, and my default size is a 16 or 18, which is good for most worsted weight yarn.

→ **Stitch markers.** I actually don't own any stitch markers, and I just use scraps of yarn instead, but stitch markers can come in handy when you work in the round or work in a circle, because it can become easy to lose your place. You can also use safety pins, dangly earrings, or slightly opened paper clips, since they are easy to get in and out of your crochet project.

→ **Small ruler or measuring tape.** This is not an essential tool, but I do have one in my kit. It comes in handy when I'm assessing gauge or measuring the finished size of my small projects.

WHAT YARN SHOULD YOU BUY?

As a beginner, you don't need to buy expensive yarn. You're probably going to make a couple of funky looking projects when you first start out, and it's better to make a $3.00 booboo than a $20.00 booboo.

I recommend that beginners start with worsted weight yarn, which is a medium weight yarn and also the weight I often work with. The plainer the better. Nothing with sequins or beads or fuzz or sparkles. Once you start to recognize what your stitches look like, you can venture into crazier yarn.

Starting from skinniest/lightest to chunkiest/heaviest, here are some of the basic yarn weights you can buy. The Craft Yarn Council developed a number system which you can find on a lot of the labels for major yarn brands like Red Heart or Lion Brand. Most of the projects in this book will use worsted weight or 4, but we will venture a little into bulkier yarn as well.

- **0** crochet thread or lace weight
- **1** fingering or sock weight
- **2** baby yarn or sport weight
- **3** DK or light worsted weight
- **4** aran or worsted weight
- **5** bulky or chunky
- **6** super bulky or roving

WHAT IS "GAUGE" AND IS IT IMPORTANT?

Gauge is the number of stitches per inch and rows per inch that result from using a certain hook size and yarn weight. Everyone's crochet style is a bit different, and you might crochet more tightly or more loosely than others. Two people who crochet with the same hook size and the same yarn weight might end up with projects of different sizes. When crocheting something like a sweater, where fit and sizing are important, you need to crochet a swatch first and check the gauge which is listed on your pattern. You might need to adjust your tension or hook size. While I do list gauges in my patterns, exact size-matching is not super essential for something like a dishcloth, so I wouldn't stress about it too much here!

HOW TO CROCHET & BASIC STITCHES

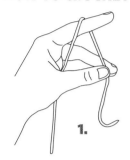

1.

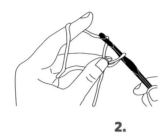

2.

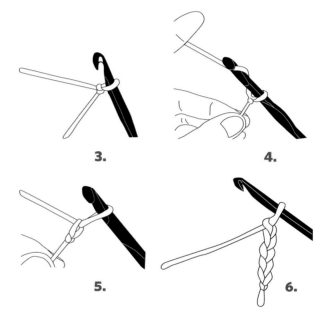

3.

4.

5.

6.

Foundation Chain (ch)

All the projects in this book begin with a foundation chain, so if you're new to crocheting, practice chaining a lot! Your goal is to keep them as uniform as possible. Also, beginners should try not to chain too tightly, since you want to be able to get your hook into the chains later on.

Step 1: Leave about 12 inches of slack in your yarn. In your left hand, place the yarn between your fourth finger and pinky, with the working yarn at the back of your hand and the 12-inch loose end coming toward you. Loop the loose end around your partially extended pointer finger, front to back. Then, hold the loose end between your thumb and third finger. This is how you will hold your yarn while you crochet. You will hook the yarn that's in the space between your pointer finger and your thumb and third finger. Your yarn will continue to feed from the back of your hand, between your ring finger and pinky. There are many variations on how to hold your yarn and hook, but this is the way that I learned! (**Fig. 1**)

Step 2: Form a slip knot any way that you like and slip it over the top of your crochet hook, or use my method as follows. Make a loop and hold it between your thumb and third finger. Stick the top of your crochet hook through the loop, hook the working

yarn (this is what we call a yarn over or yo) (**Fig. 2**), and pull it through the loop back toward you. You can tighten the slip knot and the loop around your hook by pulling on the loose and the working ends of your yarn. Make sure the loop around your hook is not too tight or you won't be able to crochet easily. (**Fig 3.**)

Step 3: Now that you have a slip knot on your hook, yo by bringing the working yarn over the hook from back to front (**Fig. 4**). Now pull your hooked yarn through the loop that was already on your hook. (**Fig. 5**) You just made your first chain. Repeat Step 3 to create as many chains as instructed. It may take some practice to keep your chains uniform, not too tight or too loose. (**Fig. 6**)

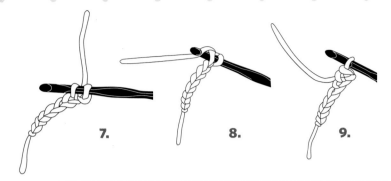

Slip Stitch (sl st)

Step 1: You should already have some foundation chains worked and a loop on your hook. Insert hook into the 2nd chain from hook. (**Fig. 7**)

Step 2: Yo and pull through both loops (the chain and the loop on your hook) (**Fig. 8 & 9**). You just made your first slip stitch. Continue to work evenly across by inserting the hook into the next chain or stitch and repeating Step 2. Word of advice: it's very easy to slip stitch too tightly, so keep it fairly loose, especially while you are learning. Use a bigger hook if you have to.

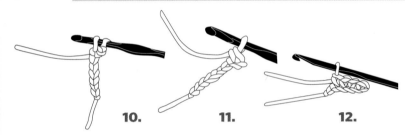

Single Crochet (sc)

Step 1: Insert your hook into the 2nd chain from your hook.

Step 2: Yo and pull your hook through the 1st loop on your hook only. (**Fig. 10**)

Step 3: Yo again and pull your hook through both loops. You just made your first single crochet stitch. Continue to work evenly across by inserting your hook into the next chain or stitch and repeating Steps 2 and 3. (**Fig. 11 & 12**)

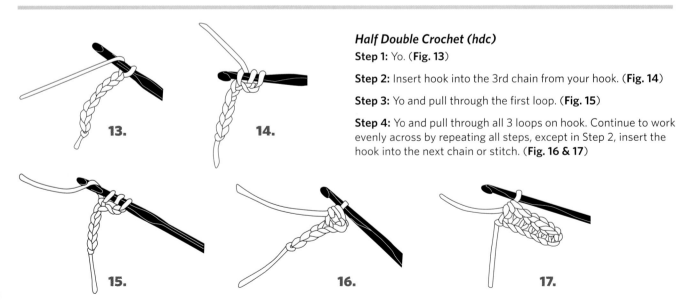

Half Double Crochet (hdc)

Step 1: Yo. (**Fig. 13**)

Step 2: Insert hook into the 3rd chain from your hook. (**Fig. 14**)

Step 3: Yo and pull through the first loop. (**Fig. 15**)

Step 4: Yo and pull through all 3 loops on hook. Continue to work evenly across by repeating all steps, except in Step 2, insert the hook into the next chain or stitch. (**Fig. 16 & 17**)

Double Crochet (dc)

Step 1: Yo.

Step 2: Insert hook into the 4th chain from hook. (**Fig. 18**)

Step 3: Yo and pull through the first loop. (**Fig. 19**)

Step 4: Yo and pull through first 2 loops on hook. (**Fig. 20**)

Step 5: Yo and pull through both loops on hook. Continue to work evenly across by repeating all steps, except in Step 2, insert hook into next chain or stitch. (**Fig. 21 & 22**)

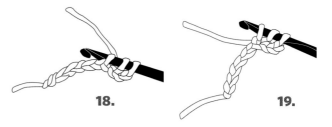

18.　　　19.

20.　　　21.　　　22.

Half Treble or Half Triple Crochet (htr)

Step 1: Yo twice. (**Fig. 23**)

Step 2: Insert hook into 5th chain from hook.

Step 3: Yo and pull through first loop.

Step 4: Yo and pull through first 2 loops.

Step 5: Yo and pull through all 3 loops on hook. Continue to work evenly across by repeating all steps, except in Step 2, insert hook into next chain or stitch. (**Fig. 24**)

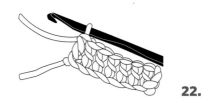

23.　　　24.

Treble or Triple Crochet (tr)

Step 1: Yo twice.

Step 2: Insert hook into 6th chain from hook.

Step 3: Yo and pull through first loop.

Step 4: Yo and pull through first 2 loops on hook.

Step 5: Yo and pull through first 2 loops on hook.

Step 6: Yo and pull through both loops on hook. Continue to work evenly across by repeating all steps, except in Step 2, insert hook into next chain or stitch. (**Fig. 25**)

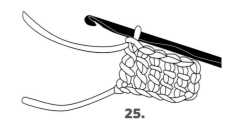

25.

Decrease by Working One Single Crochet into Next Two Stitches (sc2tog or dec)

You make the decrease by beginning the first stitch, then beginning the second stitch, and then completing both stitches at the same time as one stitch, thus creating one decrease in your stitch count. This method can be applied to hdc, dc, htr, tr, etc., as long as you remember to work two almost complete stitches before completing the last step of both simultaneously.

Also, as you continue to work into stitches from the previous row or round, you will see that there are two loops at the top of every stitch that form a "V." Unless instructed otherwise (back loop only BLO or front loop only FLO), you should generally work through both of these loops. My instructions will treat both of these loops as one loop when pulling through.

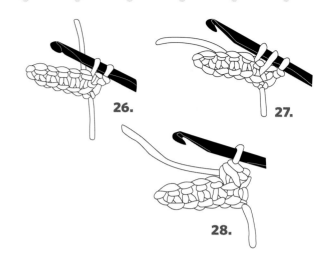

26.

27.

28.

Step 1: Insert hook into next stitch.

Step 2: Yo and pull through first loop. (**Fig. 26**)

Step 3: Insert hook into next stitch.

Step 4: Yo and pull though first loop. (**Fig. 27**)

Step 5: Yo and pull through all 3 loops. (**Fig. 28**)

Invisible Decrease (invdec)

This is actually the first way I learned to decrease, but nowadays I find it more popular for 3D work or amigurumi which are little stuffed animals. If I'm working in rows, I'll usually decrease with sc2tog. If I'm working rounds, I'll usually decrease with invdec. This also generally refers to a single crochet decrease, especially in this book, but you can use a similar method for any of the taller stitches, too. Basically, the idea is that you insert your hook into the next stitch and the following stitch at the same time, and then work one complete stitch to make the decrease.

Step 1: Insert hook into BLO or FLO of the next stitch, depending on which side of your work will be showing. If the right side (RS) —the side facing your when you work—will be showing on the outside of your finished piece, then insert hook into FLO (since the un-worked back loops will be hidden inside your project). If the wrong side (WS) - the side facing away from you when you work - will be showing on the outside of your finished piece, then insert hook into BLO (since the unworked front loops will be hidden inside your project).

Step 2: Insert hook into BLO or FLO of the following stitch (same as Step 1 but in the following stitch).

Step 3: Yo and pull through the first 2 loops.

Step 4: Yo and pull through the remaining 2 loops.

Decrease by Working One Half Double Crochet Into Next Two Stitches (hdc2tog)

Step 1: Yo and insert hook into next stitch.

Step 2: Yo and pull through first loop on hook.

Step 3: Yo and insert hook into following stitch

Step 4: Yo and pull through first loop on hook. You should now have 5 loops on your hook.

Step 5: Yo and pull through all loops on hook.

Decrease by Working One Double Crochet Into Next Two Stitches (dc2tog)

Step 1: Yo and insert hook into next stitch.

Step 2: Yo and pull through first loop on hook.

Step 3: Yo and pull through first 2 loops on hook.

Step 4: Yo and insert hook into following stitch.

Step 5: Yo and pull through first loop on hook.

Step 6: Yo and pull through first 2 loops on hook.

Step 7: Yo and pull through all loops on hook.

Work Even or Work Evenly

Continue to work in the same stitch as indicated, maintaining the same stitch count for your row or round, until you reach the end of the row or round or otherwise indicated.

Skip (sk)

Skip the next stitch or space, as indicated in the pattern.

Continuous Spiral vs. Joining Rounds

There are two ways to work "in the round" or in a circular pattern. For working in a continuous spiral, begin the next round by working the first stitch of the new round into the first stitch of the previous round. This creates a seamless project, but you should use stitch markers to keep your place. For joining after each round, you complete each round by working a slip stitch into the first stitch before beginning the next round. This creates a seam in your project, but keeping count of rounds is easier and striped work can appear neater.

Fasten Off or Break Off

When you are finished with your project, you'll have one loop left on your hook. Cut the working yarn, leaving about 6-8 inches to weave in later. Yo and pull through until the cut end of the yarn pulls through the loop. Tighten to secure.

Weave In Ends

All of the dangling yarn ends on your finished project must be neatly and invisibly woven in. I advise against tying square knots and trimming the ends short. It is highly likely that this knot will come undone and ruin all your hard work! Use your tapestry needle to pass the yarn through the inside of 4-5 stitches. If you can't see the needle on either side of your work, then you won't be able to see the yarn traveling through, either. Then change directions and weave through the inside of 4-5 stitches in the next row or round. Don't pull too tightly or warp your project. Trim the yarn. The change in direction is what really keeps the yarn tail from unraveling and popping out of your project. There are several different ways to weave in ends, but this one is my favorite.

Change Yarn Colors

Changing yarn is actually pretty intuitive. On the last stitch before your yarn or color change, work the the stitch until the last pull through. Complete that final pull through with the new yarn and then continue to work the pattern. Trim the first yarn with enough yarn tail to weave in later. I've started to change yarn by putting a slip knot on my hook in the new color and then pulling through, but this is up to you.

BASIC ABBREVIATIONS IN ALPHABETICAL ORDER

Beg: ....begin, beginning
BLO: ....back loop only
ch(s): ....chain(s)
dc: ....double crochet
dc2tog: .....double crochet 2 together
dec: ....decrease
FLO: ....front loop only
hdc: ....half double crochet
hdc2tog: ...half double crochet 2 together
htr: ....half triple or half treble crochet
invdec: ......invisible decrease
lp(s): ....loop(s)
rem: ....remaining
rep: ....repeat
rnd(s): ......round(s)
RS: ....right side
sc: ....single crochet
sc2tog: .....single crochet 2 together
sk: ....skip
sl st: ....slip stitch
st(s): ....stitch(es)
tr: ....triple crochet
WS: ....wrong side
Yo: ....yarn over
( ): ....work everything inside the parentheses in the next stitch
[ ]: ....work everything inside the brackets the number of times indicated

RESOURCES

My Favorite How-to-Crochet Websites

If you want a little more help with the basics of crochet, there are many websites that have some great instructions, including videos. Here are a few that I often tell people about.

Crafty Minx: http://www.craftyminx.com/crochet-school/
Craftsy: http://www.craftsy.com/classes/crocheting
Crochet Geek on YouTube: https://www.youtube.com/playlist
  list=PL59FA9DF4C757945B
Crochet Spot: http://www.crochetspot.com/how-to-crochet/

I also have a YouTube channel where I show you how to crochet fun projects!
http://www.youtube.com/TwinkieChanTV

Crochet Communities

Ravelry.com is a great place to find patterns—both free and for purchase—and to join groups and forums to chat about crocheting and knitting and all the projects you're working on. I have a group on Ravelry for people to ask questions and show off their finished items from my patterns: http://www.ravelry.com/groups/twinkie-chans-crochet-goodies-group

My Favorite Websites to Purchase Yarn & Supplies

I get asked a lot where I buy my yarn. You can get most of the yarn in this book from major retailers like Michaels Stores, Jo-Ann Fabrics, and Walmart, all of which have online stores as well. Here are some websites I shop at most. Also, you can Google the yarn and color you want and do some comparison shopping for the best prices.

Fabric.com: https://www.fabric.com
Jimmy Beans Wool: http://www.jimmybeanswool.com
Knit Picks: http://www.knitpicks.com
Lion Brand Yarn: http://www.lionbrand.com
Red Heart Yarn: http://www.redheart.com
Royal Yarns: http://www.royalyarns.com
Universal Yarn: http://universalyarn.com
Yarnspirations: http://www.yarnspirations.com

ACKNOWLEDGMENTS

My biggest thanks goes always to my friends, fans, and followers on social media, who leave me nice comments on my blog, give me their opinions on Facebook, let me vent on Twitter, and humor my silliness on Instagram. Without your feedback and encouragement for the past ten years (wow!), none of this would exist!

Big ups to my agent, Laura Bradford at Bradford Literary Agency. I call her Pickle, and she was once my roommate and my co-worker at the same time. She doesn't usually represent craft books, but what are friends for!? Thanks, Pickle, for sticking it out with crazy me!

Thank you to my editor Linda Neubauer at Creative Publishing international, not only for believing in my book, but especially for your unending patience and for not yelling at me. At least to my face. Do you like Edible Arrangements? What about crocheted ones? Thank you also to Regina Grenier for making the book look cute and beautiful, to Lori Steinberg for going over the patterns with a fine-toothed comb, and to Lara Neel on the marketing team for helping to get the word out.

Special shout-out to some behind-the-scenes buddies: Trista "Interro Bang Bang" for the book title—Leah Blanco Williams, who received the daunting task of being the first pair of eyeballs on my pattern drafts and cheered me on with Eye of the Tiger when I had email freak-outs about the book—Emy Kind, my lightning-fast pinch-hitter, for taking on some of the crocheting for the photos here—Marissa Barnett, for taking initial photos for the book and always being such a supportive friend—Candace Okamura, for the instructional illustrations and playing "this one or *this one*?" with me in the middle of the night when it came to any advice I needed while writing this whole thing.

All my heart to my family—Mom, Dad, Jamie, Manda. I let the book take over my life for the first two-thirds of 2015, and y'all like literally fed me. I love you and am so grateful and lucky to have such incredible support around me.

And always to Grandma Wendleton: thank you for teaching Manda and me how to crochet that day almost thirty years ago. And for calling hot dogs "wieners" and making us laugh.